BLESS YOUR HEART

BLESS ♥ YOUR ♥ HEART

*Saving the World
One Covered Dish at a Time*

WITH RECIPES BY
PATSY CALDWELL

AND STORIES BY
AMY LYLES WILSON

THOMAS NELSON
Since 1798

NASHVILLE   DALLAS   MEXICO CITY   RIO DE JANEIRO

Published in Nashville, Tennessee, by Thomas Nelson. Thomas Nelson is a registered trademark of Thomas Nelson, Inc.

Photographs by Ron Manville
Page design by Mandi Cofer

Photos on pages 14, 58, 64, 74, 84, 98, 106, 122, 128, 132, 186, 190, 192, 196, 200, 204, 210, 220, and 242 are from Shutterstock.

Photos on pages 62, 68, and 244 are from iStock.

Photo on page 206 is from Requelle Raley.

Thomas Nelson, Inc., titles may be purchased in bulk for educational, business, fund-raising, or sales promotional use. For information, please e-mail SpecialMarkets@ThomasNelson.com.

Library of Congress Cataloging-in-Publication Data

Caldwell, Patsy, 1939–
    Bless your heart : saving the world, one covered dish at a time / by Patsy Caldwell and Amy Lyles Wilson.
      p. cm.
    Includes bibliographical references and index.
    ISBN 978-1-4016-0052-5
    1. Cookery, American—Southern style. 2. Cookery—Social aspects. I. Wilson, Amy Lyles, 1961– II. Title.
TX715.2.S68C35 2010
641.5975—dc22
                                                            2010020991

Printed in the United States of America
11 12 13 14 15 16 QG 9 8 7 6 5 4

*In honor of my mother, Martha Lee Lyles Wilson, born in 1922 in
Tula, Mississippi, to Eunice and S. T. Lyles. A woman who instructed me
not to put the wooden spoon back in the cake batter after I had licked it,
and who taught me, from that day to this, how to love. And in memory
of my father, Earl Raymond Wilson (1922–2000), who introduced me
to smoked oysters and baked quail, and inspired me to live
my life not only as a dreamer but as a doer too.*

AMY LYLES WILSON

*This book is for my family—my husband Bill, my son Bryan, my daughter
Kelly and her husband Randy, and my grandchildren Scott and Paige.
And in memory of two of the best cooks I have ever known: my mother,
Irene Foster, and my next-door neighbor Mary Burton Buckner.*

PATSY CALDWELL

CONTENTS

INTRODUCTION

Southerners are good at many things. We're good at telling tales, preserving tradition, and greeting strangers on the sidewalk. We mind our manners, honor our heritage, and remember not to wear white after Labor Day. But what Southerners are really good at is food.

Just as we are instructed as children not to sass our elders, we learn early on that food is not only for eating. It is also for expressing sympathy, showing appreciation, demonstrating concern, and conveying excitement. Food that we share with others invites us to do more than ice a cake or bake a casserole. It affords us the opportunity, over and over again, to show we care.

Patsy Caldwell has felt at home in the kitchen for as long as she can remember. It started some six decades ago while standing by her mother at the stove, and has since that time led her to feed preachers, executives, politicians, athletes, and brides and grooms as a professional caterer. If you pressed her, I think Patsy would say her favorite mouths to feed are those belonging to her family. Be it her son and daughter and their families when they come for Sunday dinner, or her grandchildren when she hosts the high school seniors for a multicourse, sit-down meal, complete with candles and cloth napkins, to celebrate their proms.

"Food is at the heart of the family," says Patsy. But her idea of "family" is not limited to those she claims as kin. Patsy welcomes all comers, from the undertaker to the sheriff and anyone else who might be hungry for food and fellowship. Such hospitality epitomizes the spirit of Southern cooking in general and the philosophy of the covered dish in particular.

Although I am not as skilled in the kitchen, and I am not as quick as Patsy to invite twenty people over for dinner "just for fun," I, too, value the power of food to nourish both body and soul. Like many of you, I associate several of my life's milestones with food: my first father-daughter lunch, just the two of us, when Daddy ordered me a shrimp cocktail at the Russian Tea Room in New York while Mother was out shopping with my two older sisters; the first meal my husband made for me, which tasted not so great but showed me, at age forty-one, what true affection looks like; and the box lunches the women of my childhood church prepared for my family so we could have a bite to eat as we caravanned from the church to the cemetery, a drive of some 160 miles, to bury my father.

It's not just any kind of food, mind you, that enriches the stomach and the heart. It's the kind of food that is prepared with love. While you mix and whip and fold in, you're consoling your childhood friend, now all grown up, who has received a challenging health diagnosis. As you chop and dice and simmer, you're honoring the church organist who is retiring after fifty years in ministry. When you grease the baking dish with the butter wrapper, you're tending the elderly neighbor who doesn't get out much anymore.

Because Southerners are a humble people, we don't like to call attention to ourselves while we're working our fingers to the bone in the kitchen. Onion tears, scalded hands, and undercooked eggs are part of the territory. Don't you worry about us; we'll be fine. Making an extra casserole to put in the freezer "just in case," is what we do. It's who we are, mothers who write "big hit at potluck" on an index card before nestling it back into the recipe box. Daughters who add a note to "use more cream" in the handmade cookbook passed down from a grandmother, often a small, three-ring binder full of notes and recipes and newspaper clippings. Such scribblings are more than suggestions for how to cook; they are instructions on how to live.

Regardless of your culinary skills or your food preferences, what it comes down to is this: What might look like a simple chicken potpie sustains the friend who had surgery last week. That strawberry cake you've made a hundred times reassures your elderly aunt that she has not been forgotten even though she can't make it out to the family reunions anymore. Whatever you do, don't underestimate the power of the covered dish to celebrate, commiserate, and console. Maybe it can even save the world.

It is our hope that you will take and eat—and share—from *Bless Your Heart*, secure in the knowledge that when you feed someone you give one of the greatest gifts a person has to offer: yourself.

Amy Lyles Wilson

♥ CHAPTER 1 ♥

CHURCH POTLUCK

FEEDING THE FAITHFUL

My friend Betty Love likes to say the church taught her to love the Lord and the church potluck taught her to respect a perfectly shaped gelatin mold. (Our neighbor Charlotte insists it's called "Add a Dish," but she's from a really small town Betty Love and I have never heard of.)

As a teenager, Betty Love was charged with helping her mother prepare food for the monthly church potluck. Her father was head deacon, so they were expected to do more than chop up a head of iceberg and call it a salad. And her mother said it would be "sinful" to pick up a couple of pies at the Piggy Wiggly and pretend they had baked them.

"Get it?" she would ask Betty Love, smiling. "Sinful!"

"I spent more hours than I can remember," says Betty Love, "helping my parents haul tuna noodle casseroles, fruit salads with and without poppy seed dressing on account of Mrs. Miles and her finicky dentures, and carrot cakes with half-inch-thick cream cheese icing to the fellowship hall of the First Millerville Anointed Redeemer Church.

"There I'd be," she says, "in the back seat of the station wagon, balancing this concoction or that in my lap while Daddy kept eyeing me in the rearview mirror, checking to see if anything had tipped over and if I had thought to bring a dish towel just in case. I never spilled a drop, because Daddy always drove about fifteen miles an hour and kept his hands at ten and two."

Sometimes Betty Love pauses about now to take a breath before continuing. "The worst was when Mother decided to take more food than usual, and I was forced to steady a pan on the floor between my penny loafers and keep my little brother from swiping his index finger through the icing for a lick. Every month, just as we were pulling into the parking lot of the church, my parents wondered aloud if the preacher's wife would have the nerve to show up with yet another batch of salmon croquettes.

"'Surely this time she'll bring something different,' my mother would say.

"'Surely,' echoed my father. And every month, there they were, laid out like an overcooked, sacrificial offering atop the long folding table: two layers of round patties, blackened on both sides and pinkish-orange in the middle."

Betty Love makes a funny face when she gets to this point in the story, as if to emphasize the awfulness.

"We had no idea what salmon croquettes were, only that they went down better with lots of ketchup. Daddy made us eat them, of course, so as not to offend the preacher, or, even worse, the preacher's wife. So we swallowed fast and prayed we wouldn't gag on a bit of fishbone."

Betty Love was well into her thirties before she realized not every church subscribes to the potluck theory of feeding the faithful. When she moved away to take a job in Louisiana, she attended a church that served catered food. Where's the faith in that, Betty Love wants to know? Just as the Lord invites everyone to the table, the potluck makes room for all manner and degree of cooking skills and imagination. While one believer may think his tofu chili with extra jalapeños is heavenly, his fellow pilgrim might consider hot and spicy as evidence that the devil is indeed alive and well. The "anything goes" approach of the potluck implies that whatever is provided will be acceptable and appreciated. Which brings us to Mrs. Jenkins and her chipped beef on toast.

One year everybody got sick as dogs within hours of the potluck and although no one can be sure, the bulk of the aspersion was cast squarely toward the Jenkins's kitchen.

"Mother had been over there once for a Circle meeting," says Betty Love, "and she just happened to notice that the drip pans on the stove were stained and there was a funny smell coming from the crisper in the refrigerator. She never looked at Mrs. Jenkins quite the same way again."

Oh the stories Betty Love could tell! Back in 1992, there was a disproportionate number of yellow vegetables and frozen salads that October when her mother was in bed with a bad back and someone else, probably Mrs. Jenkins now that she thinks about it, took over as temporary chairwoman of the potluck committee. And how one time the choir director claimed he put plenty of real sugar in the iced tea, but everyone knew it was artificial sweetener because he was trying to lose weight before the upcoming choral competition over in Chapel Hill, and so some of the congregants drank grape juice from the communion closet instead. But Betty Love was raised right, so she won't say another word.

Taking a covered dish to church for a potluck—or "Add a Dish" or "Meal Day," depending on where you hail from—is an obligation for some, an initiation into a new faith community for others, and a way of life for a lot of us. Be it to welcome a new preacher, honor a congregant who's turning ninety, celebrate a holiday, or convene the annual meeting, such sharing of food with friend and visitor alike is surely a kind of communion.

Grape Tea

This delicious tea will keep for a week if everyone doesn't drink it all up the first day. It never lasts a week around my house.

    ½   cup instant tea mix
        Lemonade mix, enough to make a gallon
        (can use sweetened or unsweetened)
    3   cups white grape juice
    1 ½ cups sugar
    12 cups water

Mix the tea, lemonade mix, grape juice, and sugar together in a gallon container.

Add the water to make one gallon, stirring well until combined. Keep refrigerated.

Makes 10 servings.

Kitchen Sink Broccoli Corn Muffins

This corn bread muffin gets its name because it seems to have everything in it but the kitchen sink. But the little extra work is so worth it.

    1   (10-ounce) package frozen chopped broccoli, thawed and drained
    2   tablespoons onion, finely chopped
    ¾   cup small curd cottage cheese
    ½   cup butter, melted
    4   large eggs, slightly beaten
    ½   teaspoon salt
    ½   cup shredded cheddar cheese
    ⅓   cup buttermilk
    1   (8-ounce) package corn muffin mix

Preheat the oven to 400 degrees. Grease 18 standard-size muffin tin cups. In a large bowl combine the broccoli, onion, cottage cheese, butter, eggs, salt, cheese, and the buttermilk. Mix well. Add the corn muffin mix, stirring just to combine. Fill each muffin cup ⅔ full. Bake for 20 minutes.

Makes 18 muffins.

Southern Spoon Rolls

If you don't want to use all of the dough this recipe makes at one time, you can place it in an airtight bowl and it will keep in the refrigerator for 3 to 4 days.

¾ cup butter, melted
¼ cup sugar
2 cups warm water, divided
1 large egg, slightly beaten
1 package active dry yeast
4 cups self-rising flour

Preheat the oven to 400 degrees. Grease two 12-cup muffin tins. In a large bowl mix the butter, sugar, and 1 ¾ cups of the water. Add the beaten egg and stir. In a small bowl add the remaining ¼ cup water and the yeast and stir to dissolve. Add the dissolved yeast to the sugar mixture and stir. Add the flour and stir until well mixed. Drop by spoonfuls into the prepared muffin tins. Bake for 20 minutes or until golden brown.

Makes 2 dozen rolls.

Macaroni and Cheese with Cream of Mushroom Soup

2 (10.75-ounce) cans cream of mushroom soup
2 cups milk
1 pound shredded cheddar cheese plus 1 cup, divided
½ cup American cheese
¼ cup grated Parmesan cheese
1 pound macaroni, cooked according to package directions and drained

Preheat the oven to 350 degrees. Grease a 13 x 9-inch baking dish. In a large saucepan over medium heat mix the mushroom soup, milk, 1 pound of the cheddar cheese, the American cheese, and Parmesan cheese together, stirring until the cheeses melt. Remove from the heat and stir in the macaroni. Pour into the prepared casserole dish. Sprinkle the remaining 1 cup of cheddar cheese over the top. Bake for 30 minutes or until the mixture is bubbly and the cheese is golden brown.

Makes 10 to 12 servings.

"I Hope the Sermon Isn't Too Long" Oven-Roasted Beef Tenderloin

You can put this dish in the oven when you leave for church and it will be ready to take out of the oven when you get home. That is, as long as you don't have a long-winded preacher.

- ¼ cup chopped parsley
- 2 teaspoons minced garlic
- 1 tablespoon paprika
- 1 ½ teaspoons dry mustard
- 2 tablespoons coarse salt
- ½ teaspoon cayenne pepper
- 2 tablespoons black pepper
- 1 (4-pound) beef tenderloin, trimmed of excess fat
- 2 tablespoons olive oil

Preheat the oven to 250 degrees. In a small bowl add the parsley, garlic, paprika, dry mustard, salt, cayenne pepper, and black pepper and mix well. Brush the tenderloin with the oil. Press the rub on all sides of the meat. Let stand at room temperature for 40 minutes before cooking. Cook the tenderloin for 1 ½ to 2 hours. Check with a meat thermometer in the thickest part for a reading of 130 degrees for rare. Remove to a carving board, cover with foil, and let rest 30 minutes.

To serve: slice ½-inch-thick pieces for a main course, thinner if you are planning to serve on rolls.

Makes 10 servings or 30 beef and roll sandwiches.

Billy's South of the Border Chili

*My brother Billy is the most gracious host. He and his wife, Wilma, served this the last time
I visited them.*

    2   pounds ground chuck or ground round beef
    1   cup diced onion
    2   (1.25-ounce) packages taco seasoning mix
    2   cups water
    1   (15-ounce) can diced tomatoes
    1   (10-ounce) can chopped tomatoes and green chilies
    1   (15-ounce) can tomato sauce
    1   (4-ounce) can mushroom pieces, do not drain
    1   (15-ounce) can whole kernel corn
    2   (15-ounce) cans pinto beans, do not drain
        Salt to taste
        Cheddar cheese, sour cream, and green onions for topping (optional)

Place a 4-quart Dutch oven over medium to medium-high heat. When the pan is hot add the
ground beef and stir, breaking up the meat. Continue to cook until all the pink is gone. Add
the onion and cook until transparent. Add the taco seasoning, water, diced tomatoes, chopped
tomatoes and green chilies, and tomato sauce and simmer for 30 minutes. Add the mushroom
pieces, corn, and pinto beans. Simmer for an additional 45 minutes. Add salt to taste.

   To serve: top with cheddar cheese, sour cream, and green onions if desired.

Makes 8 servings.

Baked Spaghetti

Be prepared. People will ask you for the recipe when you take this to a potluck.

1 ¼	pounds ground beef (I prefer ground chuck.)
½	cup finely chopped onion
1	teaspoon minced garlic
1	(14.25-ounce) can diced tomatoes
1	(10-ounce) can tomatoes and green chilies
1	(4-ounce) can sliced mushrooms, drained
½	cup stuffed olives, thinly sliced
1	teaspoon salt
½	teaspoon black pepper
1	pound American cheese, grated (You can also use processed cheese spread.)
½	pound thin spaghetti, cooked and drained according to package directions

Preheat the oven to 350 degrees. Prepare a 13 x 9-inch baking dish by spraying with nonstick cooking spray. Brown the ground beef in a large saucepan over medium to high heat. When lightly brown add the chopped onion and garlic. Continue cooking for about 5 minutes. Add the diced tomatoes, tomatoes and green chilies, mushrooms, olives, salt, and pepper. Mix thoroughly. Add the cheese and spaghetti. Stir until the cheese melts. Place in the prepared baking dish. Bake for 20 to 25 minutes or until bubbly.

Makes 8 servings.

Orange Sherbet Salad with Ambrosia

Salad:
2 (3-ounce) packages orange gelatin
2 cups boiling water
1 pint orange sherbet
1 (11-ounce) can mandarin oranges, drained

Ambrosia:
1 (11-ounce) can mandarin oranges, drained
1 (20-ounce) can crushed pineapple, drained
1 cup flaked coconut
½ cup maraschino cherries
½ cup chopped pecans
1 cup sour cream
1 cup miniature marshmallows

To make the salad: In a large bowl place the gelatin and add the boiling water, stirring to dissolve. Add the sherbet and mix until it melts. Chill until partially set. Add the mandarin oranges. Spray a 2-quart ring mold with vegetable spray and pour the gelatin mixture into the ring mold. Place in the refrigerator for at least 8 hours before serving.

To make the ambrosia: Combine the oranges, pineapple, coconut, cherries, pecans, sour cream, and marshmallows in a large bowl. Cover and chill for 8 hours.

To serve: Unmold the orange sherbet salad onto a serving plate. Fill the center with the ambrosia.

Makes 10 servings.

Twice As Nice Baked Potatoes

These are always a big hit.

6 medium baking potatoes
½ cup butter
1 cup grated cheddar cheese
1 teaspoon salt
½ teaspoon black pepper
½ cup sour cream
½ to 1 cup milk
4 slices bacon, cooked and crumbled (optional)
½ cup chopped green onions (optional)

Preheat the oven to 400 degrees. Scrub the potatoes and place them on a large baking pan. Bake for 1 hour or until the potatoes test tender when pricked with the point of a knife. Split the warm potatoes in half lengthwise, and carefully scoop out the pulp, leaving the shells intact. Combine the potato pulp with the butter, cheese, salt, pepper, and sour cream. Using a mixer, mix well. Add the milk as needed. Stuff the shells with the potato mixture. Bake at 400 degrees for 15 to 20 minutes or until golden brown. Top with the crumbled bacon and chopped green onions if desired.

Makes 12 servings.

Norma's Pretzel Salad

This recipe came from one of the dearest ladies I have ever had the pleasure to know. She is no longer with us, but we serve this recipe almost every time our family gathers together.

2 ½   cups pretzels
¾   cup butter, melted
1   cup plus 3 tablespoons sugar, divided
1   (8-ounce) package cream cheese, softened
1   (8-ounce) carton frozen whipped topping, thawed
1   (6-ounce) package strawberry gelatin
2   cups boiling water
2   (10-ounce) packages frozen sliced strawberries

To make the first layer: Preheat the oven to 400 degrees. In a food processor, pulse the pretzels, butter, and 3 tablespoons of the sugar until the mixture resembles coarse sand. Press the mixture into a 13 x 9-inch dish. Bake for 8 minutes. Cool thoroughly.

To make the second layer: Mix the softened cream cheese and the remaining 1 cup sugar together. Fold in the thawed whipped topping. Spread over the cooled pretzel layer.

To make the third layer: Dissolve the strawberry gelatin in the boiling water. Add the frozen strawberries. Chill until syrupy and then pour over the cream cheese layer. Refrigerate for at least 4 hours.

Makes 12 servings.

NOTE: This can be made a day ahead.

Deviled Eggs

Maybe the only time the devil is welcome at church.

- 6 large eggs
- 3 tablespoons mayonnaise
- 2 teaspoons Dijon mustard
- ½ teaspoon salt
- ¼ teaspoon black pepper
- 1 teaspoon vinegar
- 4 drops Tabasco
- Paprika, for garnish

Place the eggs in a saucepan large enough to accommodate all of the eggs in a single layer, covering with water by 1 inch. Simmer over medium heat for 14 minutes. Remove from heat and place the eggs in cold water to prevent further cooking. Crack the shells, peel and split lengthwise. Remove the yolks, place in a small bowl, and mash with a fork. Add the mayonnaise, mustard, salt, black pepper, vinegar, and hot sauce and mix well. Spoon the filling into the whites. Garnish with paprika.

Makes 12 servings.

Chicken Casserole with Asparagus and Almonds

1 (15-ounce) can asparagus spears, drained
3 (5-ounce) chicken breasts, boiled until tender, drained, and chopped
1 (10.75-ounce) can cream of chicken soup
½ cup mayonnaise
2 teaspoons lemon juice
¾ cup grated cheddar cheese
½ cup slivered almonds
1 cup butter cracker crumbs

Preheat the oven to 350 degrees. Grease a 9-inch-square baking dish. Layer the asparagus in the prepared baking dish and add the chopped chicken on top. In a small bowl combine the cream of chicken soup, mayonnaise, lemon juice, cheese, and almonds and pour over the chicken. Sprinkle with the cracker crumbs and bake for 30 minutes.

Makes 6 servings.

Green Beans with Chili Sauce

For such an easy dish to make, this is full of flavor.

2 tablespoons cooking oil or bacon drippings
½ cup onion, minced
1 (28-ounce) can French-style green beans, drained
½ cup chili sauce

Place a 2-quart saucepan over medium heat. Add the oil or bacon drippings and the onion and sauté for 3 minutes. Add the green beans and chili sauce. Cover and simmer for 30 minutes.

Makes 6 servings.

Jam Cake with Easy Caramel Icing

If you can't find pear honey, you can substitute ½ cup strawberry preserves.

Jam cake:
- ½ cup butter, softened
- 1 cup sugar
- 3 large eggs, separated
- 1 teaspoon baking soda
- ½ cup buttermilk
- 1 ½ cups all-purpose flour
- ½ teaspoon cinnamon
- ½ teaspoon nutmeg
- ½ teaspoon cloves
- ½ teaspoon allspice
- 1 ½ tablespoons cocoa powder
- 1 cup blackberry jam
- ½ cup pear honey
- ½ cup raisins
- ½ cup chopped pecans

Caramel icing:
- 2 cups sugar
- ½ cup buttermilk
- 1 teaspoon baking soda
- 3 tablespoons light corn syrup
- ½ cup butter
- 1 teaspoon vanilla extract

To make the jam cake: Preheat the oven to 350 degrees. Grease and flour three 8-inch round cake pans. In the bowl of your electric mixer combine the butter and sugar. Add the egg yolks one at a time, mixing well after each addition. In a small bowl combine the baking soda and buttermilk and set aside. In another small bowl combine the flour, cinnamon, nutmeg, cloves, allspice, and cocoa powder. Alternately add the spice and buttermilk mixtures to the creamed mixture, beginning and ending with the dry mix. Add the jam, pear honey, raisins, and pecans.

In a medium bowl whip the egg whites until soft peaks form. Fold the whites into the cake batter. Divide the batter equally among the prepared pans. Bake for 25 to 30 minutes. The cakes are done when a toothpick comes out clean when inserted into the middle of each pan. Let the cakes cool in the pans for 10 minutes. Turn out onto waxed paper and let cool completely before icing.

To make the caramel icing: In a large saucepan combine the sugar and buttermilk. Add the baking soda, corn syrup, and butter. Cook over medium heat, stirring constantly until the mixture forms a soft ball stage (238 degrees). Remove from the heat and add the vanilla. Let cool for 10 minutes. Beat with a wooden spoon until the icing achieves spreading consistency. Divide among the 3 layers, icing the tops and sides.

Makes 16 servings.

Peanut Butter Meringue Pie

If ever there was an event you should take this pie to, a church potluck would be it. Why? Because this pie is pretty close to heaven on earth.

Filling:
- ½ cup sugar
- 3 tablespoons cornstarch
- 1 ½ tablespoons all-purpose flour
- ⅓ teaspoon salt
- 3 egg yolks
- 3 cups milk
- 1 tablespoon butter
- 1 teaspoon vanilla extract
- ½ cup peanut butter (crunchy or creamy)
- ¾ cup powdered sugar
- 1 (9-inch) piecrust, baked according to package directions

Meringue:
- 3 egg whites
- ¼ teaspoon cream of tartar
- ¼ cup sugar

To make the filling: In a large saucepan mix the sugar, cornstarch, flour, and salt. In a medium bowl lightly beat the egg yolks and combine with the milk. Pour the egg mixture into the saucepan. Cook over medium heat until thick, stirring constantly. Remove from the heat and add the butter and vanilla. In a small bowl use your fingers to mix the peanut butter and powdered sugar together, until the mixture is crumbly.

To assemble the pie, divide the peanut butter crumbs into 3 equal portions. Place ⅓ of the crumbs on top of the piecrust. Pour ½ of the filling over the crumbs. Place the second batch of crumbs over the filling and top with the remaining filling. Reserve the third batch of crumbs for the meringue.

To prepare the meringue: Preheat the oven to 350 degrees. In the bowl of an electric mixer beat the egg whites and cream of tartar until soft peaks form. Gradually add the sugar, continuing to beat until stiff peaks form. Spread on top of the pie filling and sprinkle with the third batch of peanut butter crumbs. Bake for 10 minutes or until golden brown.

Makes 1 pie or 6 to 8 servings.

Mother's Banana Blueberry Pie

My mother made this very simple pie for my family on many occasions. I think of her every time I make this.

1   (8-ounce) package cream cheese, softened
1   cup sugar
1   (8-ounce) package frozen whipped topping, thawed
4   medium-size bananas
2   (9-inch) baked pie shells
1   (20-ounce) can blueberry pie filling

In a large bowl combine the softened cream cheese and sugar. Fold the thawed whipped topping into the cream cheese mixture. Slice the bananas and place them in the bottoms of the 2 piecrusts, being careful not to overlap the slices. Pour the cream cheese mixture over the bananas. Chill for 3 hours and top with the blueberry pie filling.

Makes 2 pies or 12 to 16 servings.

Temptation Carrot-Pineapple Cake with Cream Cheese Icing

Blessed are those children who can pass this cake by before it has been sliced—without being tempted to run a finger through the frosting to get a taste.

Cake:
- 2 cups self-rising flour
- 2 teaspoons cinnamon
- 1 ½ cups vegetable oil
- 2 cups sugar
- 4 large eggs, slightly beaten
- 2 cups carrots, finely grated
- 1 (8-ounce) can crushed pineapple
- ¾ cup chopped pecans

Cream cheese icing:
- 1 (8-ounce) package cream cheese, softened
- ½ cup butter
- 1 pound powdered sugar
- 1 teaspoon vanilla extract
- ½ cup chopped pecans

To make the cake: Preheat the oven to 325 degrees. Grease and flour two 9-inch round cake pans. In a medium bowl mix the flour and cinnamon. In a large bowl combine the oil, sugar, and eggs and mix well. Add the flour mixture and continue beating to blend ingredients. Fold in the carrots, pineapple, and pecans. Pour the cake batter into the prepared pans. Bake for approximately 50 minutes or until a toothpick inserted into the center of each pan comes out clean. Cool for 10 minutes. Remove from the pans and cool completely before icing.

To make the cream cheese icing: In the bowl of an electric mixer combine the cream cheese and butter. Add the powdered sugar and vanilla, beating until creamy. Fold in the pecans. Spread the icing over the top of each layer, stacking one on top of the other. Ice the sides.

Makes 16 servings.

Double Treat Chocolate Pecan Bars

Forrest Gump thought things went together like peas and carrots. For me, it's chocolate and pecans.

3	cups all-purpose flour
2	cups sugar, divided
1	cup butter, softened
½	teaspoon salt
1 ½	cups corn syrup, dark or light
1	cup semisweet chocolate chips
4	eggs, slightly beaten
1	teaspoon vanilla extract
2	cups chopped pecans

Preheat the oven to 350 degrees. Grease a 15 x 10-inch baking pan. In a large bowl add the flour, ¾ cup of the sugar, butter, and salt. Mix on medium speed until it becomes crumbly. Press dough firmly into the prepared pan and bake for 20 minutes.

While the crust is baking, prepare the filling. In a medium saucepan over low heat cook the corn syrup and chocolate chips, stirring until the chocolate melts. Remove from the heat and add the remaining 1 ¼ cups sugar, eggs, vanilla, and pecans. Stir until well blended. Pour the filling over the hot crust. Return to the oven and bake for 30 more minutes. Cool for 1 hour before cutting into bars.

Makes 4 dozen bars.

♥ CHAPTER 2 ♥

BODY AND SOUL

WHEN WORDS AREN'T ENOUGH

Aunt Lutie can't remember when she started calling the funeral home hotlines every morning, but she can tell you exactly when her tireless and selfless dedication to her community began to yield fruit.

"January 18, 2005," she says. "Eddie Ray Barnell, ninety-two, dropped dead in the middle of the night on a Saturday. Heart attack in the backyard. He was in his bare feet, and to this day his wife says she has no idea why he went outside. Some of us have our suspicions, but we don't like to talk out of turn.

"Of course the editor down at the *Gazette* couldn't have known to anticipate it before the last edition of the week on Friday. I was the first one out to the Barnell place with my mixed medley casserole. Serves ten. Twelve if you don't spoon out big portions, and I knew it would be a small crowd at the house because the Barnells, bless their hearts, never had any children."

Aunt Lutie always keeps at least one casserole in the freezer, along with a small loaf or two of banana nut bread, in order to be prepared at all times for just such unfortunate situations. But when time allows, she likes to start from scratch. It seems more compassionate, she thinks, and it gives her an edge over the competition now that Louise from the post office has started calling the hotlines too.

"But everyone knows I was the first one to think of it, and Louise's memory is slipping," says Aunt Lutie, standing up just a little taller and smoothing down her housecoat with pride when she speaks of her industrious nature. She doesn't like to brag, of course; just set the record straight is all.

"Louise never remembers to call the hotlines on the weekends, and most days she forgets that Oddfellows Funeral Parlor is not the only game in town anymore. And anyway, nobody likes that 'Brussels sprouts supreme' of hers. Louise says it's an 'acquired taste,' but I have yet to meet anyone who's 'acquired' it, especially when mired in the throes of grief."

Aunt Lutie believes with all her heart that what people need in such a trying time is food they can count on, food that doesn't confuse them, or taste funny, or threaten to cause them indigestion. It's the least you can do for someone who has just lost a loved one.

"When my beloved Pete passed," Aunt Lutie says, "I about keeled over myself when Myra Sullivan had the gall to leave a thermos of clam chowder on my front porch with a note that read, 'a little something to warm your soul.' I can't think of one time in my seventy-four years on this earth when clams have warmed my soul, and you can bet your life that was canned soup. She might have added one of those small cartons of whipping cream, but I doubt it. No wonder she didn't want to show her face inside the house."

Aunt Lutie takes her mission seriously. It's not a role assigned to her by anyone local, mind you, as Aunt Lutie gets her marching orders from the Lord. In fact, she is so intent on spreading solace through cooking that she doesn't always stop to think if her efforts will be welcome. Like the time she showed up at a funeral home over in Atlanta for the visitation of a woman she had met recently on a church retreat. The "Senior Singles Spiritual Salvation Weekend" turned out to be a little too evangelical for Aunt Lutie, but she was thankful for two days in the mountains nonetheless.

To no avail, Aunt Lutie looked hither and yon throughout the sprawling funeral home for the kitchen or a meeting room so that she might add her pies to the other covered dishes brought by the mourners. Several people stared at her blankly when she inquired, so she finally returned the pies to the towel on the back seat of her Buick before trying again to sign the guest book and pay her respects to the dead woman's children.

"Ne'er do wells," the woman had said when talking about them with Aunt Lutie at the retreat, but Aunt Lutie thought they deserved a hug at least, seeing that they wouldn't get to eat her pies.

"What kind of people don't bring food to visitation?" says Aunt Lutie, still incredulous several months after the fact. "The grieving family needs to keep up their strength."

Stunned but not defeated, Aunt Lutie decided to swing by the Happy Trails Retirement Village on her way back to town. She knew in her heart that someone needed what she had to give. It wasn't just anybody who could roll out a crust with such finesse that it baked up firm *and* flaky. But Aunt Lutie could. It was a gift. Maybe not an official "fruit of the spirit" like those outlined by St. Paul, she'll grant you that. But a gift nonetheless.

So she would search out those who were hurting—and hungry—and offer them a slice of sweet relief. With any luck, they would take and eat and feel a little better, and the good Lord would be able to say of Aunt Lutie yet again, "Well done, my good and faithful servant."

Strawberry Iced Tea

This is a wonderfully refreshing iced tea.

⅓ cup instant tea
5 cups water
1 (12-ounce) can frozen lemonade concentrate, thawed
1 (16-ounce) package frozen sliced strawberries, thawed and pureed
1 (12-ounce) can ginger ale

In a large pitcher combine the tea, water, lemonade, and pureed strawberries. Add the ginger ale and stir well. Chill and serve over ice.

Makes 8 servings.

Country-style Steak

The gravy this dish makes is delicious on top of mashed potatoes.

1 ½ to 2 pounds round steak, sliced ½-inch thick
1 teaspoon salt
1 teaspoon black pepper
½ cup plus 3 tablespoons all-purpose flour
¼ cup canola oil
½ medium onion, thinly sliced
1 (4-ounce) can sliced mushrooms, drained
4 cups water

Preheat the oven to 325 degrees. Grease a 13 x 9-inch baking dish. Cut the steak into 6 to 8 serving pieces and season with salt and pepper. In a shallow dish add ½ cup of the flour and dredge the steak. In a 9-inch skillet heat the oil over medium heat. When the oil is hot, brown each piece of meat and set aside in the prepared baking dish. Pour off all but 3 tablespoons of the pan drippings. Add the remaining 3 tablespoons flour to the pan, stirring to remove any brown bits. Add the sliced onion and stir to cook for 2 minutes. Add the mushrooms and water. Continue to cook and stir to blend, bring to a boil and cook for 3 minutes more. Pour the gravy over the meat. Cover with foil. Place in the oven for 3 hours or until tender.

Makes 6 servings.

Skillet Pineapple Upside-Down Cake

Telling this will be showing my age, but this is the first cake I remember my mother making. We didn't have cake pans, so she made this in a cast-iron skillet.

2	tablespoons butter
½	cup firmly packed brown sugar
1	(20-ounce) can pineapple slices, drained
	Maraschino cherries (optional)
3	large eggs, separated
1 ½	cups sugar, divided
1 ½	cups cake flour, sifted
1	teaspoon baking powder
¼	teaspoon salt
½	cup boiling water

Preheat the oven to 350 degrees. In a 10-inch cast-iron skillet melt the butter over low heat. Sprinkle the brown sugar evenly over the butter and remove from the heat. Arrange the pineapple slices in a single layer over the brown sugar mixture. Place a maraschino cherry in the center of each of the pineapple rings, if desired. Set aside.

In a large bowl beat the egg yolks with a mixer on medium speed until thick, about 5 minutes. Gradually add ½ cup of the sugar, beating well. In a medium bowl combine the flour, the remaining 1 cup sugar, baking powder, and salt. Add the flour mixture and the boiling water to the egg mixture, alternately, beginning and ending with the flour. In a separate mixing bowl, beat the egg whites on high speed until stiff peaks form. Carefully fold the whites into the batter. Spoon the batter evenly over the pineapple slices.

Bake for 45 minutes. Immediately invert cake onto a serving plate.

Makes 10 servings.

Blue Cheese Drop Biscuits

These biscuits are wonderful with beef tenderloin and brisket.

- 2 ½ cups all-purpose flour
- 2 teaspoons baking powder
- 2 tablespoons sugar
- ½ teaspoon salt
- 6 tablespoons butter, cubed
- 1 to 1 ½ cups heavy cream
- 2 large eggs
- ¼ cup crumbled blue cheese

Preheat the oven to 375 degrees. Lightly grease a baking sheet. In a large bowl combine the flour, baking powder, sugar, and salt. Cut the butter into the flour mixture. In a small bowl combine the cream, eggs, and blue cheese and add to the dry mixture, stirring to mix. Scoop the biscuit dough onto the prepared baking sheet with a 2-ounce ice cream scoop. Bake for 15 to 20 minutes or until golden brown.

Makes 16 biscuits.

Cheesy Baked Zucchini

In the South, the only thing that grows faster than kudzu is zucchini. This recipe is one great use for it.

2	pounds zucchini, sliced ¼-inch thick
1	cup finely chopped onion
½	cup shredded Swiss cheese
1	cup shredded cheddar cheese
1	(4-ounce) can chopped green chilies
½	cup sour cream
½	teaspoon salt
½	teaspoon black pepper
1	cup Ritz cracker crumbs
½	cup grated Parmesan cheese
2	tablespoons butter

Preheat the oven to 350 degrees. Grease a 13 x 9-inch baking dish. Place the zucchini and onion with enough water to cover by 1 inch in a large saucepan and cook for about 10 minutes or until tender. Drain and place in the prepared dish. In a small bowl combine the Swiss cheese, cheddar cheese, green chilies, sour cream, salt, and pepper. Spread over the zucchini. In a small bowl mix the Ritz cracker crumbs and Parmesan cheese. Sprinkle the cracker mixture on top of the casserole and dot with the butter. Bake for 25 minutes.

Makes 8 servings.

Sweet Enough to Eat Sweet Potato Casserole

You could almost use this as a dessert. But why would you not want to have some cake too?

Sweet potatoes:

- 2 cups mashed sweet potatoes (1 [28-ounce] can sweet potatoes, drained; or 3 medium sweet potatoes, baked and mashed)
- 1 ¼ cups sugar
- 2 large eggs, beaten
- 12 tablespoons melted butter, divided
- 1 cup milk
- ½ teaspoon nutmeg
- ½ teaspoon cinnamon

Topping:

- ¾ cup crushed corn flakes
- ½ cup chopped pecans
- ½ cup firmly packed brown sugar

Preheat the oven to 400 degrees. Grease a 13 x 9-inch baking dish. In a large bowl combine the sweet potatoes, sugar, eggs, 6 tablespoons of the melted butter, milk, nutmeg, and cinnamon. Mix well and pour into the baking dish. Bake for 20 minutes.

While the sweet potatoes are baking, prepare the topping. In a small bowl combine the corn flakes, pecans, brown sugar, and the remaining 6 tablespoons melted butter. Sprinkle on top of the baked sweet potatoes and bake for an additional 10 minutes. Serve hot.

Makes 12 servings.

Cabbage Slaw with Red and Green Apples

If there is a prettier slaw than this, I haven't seen it. It's delicious too.

- 1 medium head of cabbage, shredded (about 8 cups)
- 1 large red apple, unpeeled, cored and diced
- 1 large green apple, unpeeled, cored and diced
- 1 cup toasted slivered almonds
- 1 cup dried cranberries
- ½ cup mayonnaise
- ½ cup sour cream
- ½ teaspoon salt
- ½ teaspoon black pepper

In a large bowl mix the cabbage, red and green apples, almonds, and cranberries. In a small bowl combine the mayonnaise, sour cream, salt, and pepper. Combine the mayonnaise mixture with the cabbage mixture. Refrigerate for 2 hours before serving.

Makes 10 servings.

Corn Light Bread

In the South we call white bread, "light bread." The recipe is exactly what the name implies—half corn bread, half light bread.

- 2 cups plain (white) cornmeal
- ½ cup all-purpose flour
- ¾ cup sugar
- ½ teaspoon baking soda
- 1 teaspoon salt
- 1 package active dry yeast
- 2 cups buttermilk
- 3 tablespoons vegetable oil

Preheat the oven to 375 degrees. Grease a 9 x 5 x 3-inch loaf pan. In a medium bowl combine the cornmeal, flour, sugar, baking soda, salt, and dry yeast. Add the buttermilk and oil, mixing well. Pour into the prepared pan. Bake for 45 to 50 minutes or until firm to the touch and golden brown.

Makes 8 servings.

Hamburger Stroganoff

Talk about quick and delicious. You can have this ready to go in less than half an hour if you are late hearing the news about someone's passing.

¼ cup butter

½ cup minced onion

1 teaspoon minced garlic

1 pound ground beef (preferably ground chuck)

2 tablespoons all-purpose flour

2 teaspoons salt

½ teaspoon black pepper

1 (8-ounce) can sliced mushrooms, drained

1 (10 ¾–ounce) can condensed cream of chicken soup

1 cup sour cream

In a large skillet melt the butter. Sauté the onion and garlic until they are translucent. Add the ground beef to the onion and garlic mixture, stirring as the beef browns. Add the flour, salt, pepper, and mushrooms. Cook for 5 minutes, continuing to stir. Add the soup and simmer uncovered for 10 minutes. Stir in the sour cream. Heat thoroughly. Serve over rice or noodles.

Makes 6 servings.

Carrots with Walnuts and Honey

Cooked carrots are one of our most forgotten vegetables. Too often we think they should only be eaten raw or in salads. This recipe will change your mind.

6	cups baby carrots
1 ½	cups water
1 ½	teaspoons salt, divided
½	cup butter, melted
1	tablespoon honey
½	teaspoon black pepper
2	tablespoons lemon juice
⅔	cup walnuts, coarsely chopped

Place the carrots in a medium saucepan. Add the water and ½ teaspoon of the salt. Cover and cook over medium heat for about 6 minutes or until tender. Drain thoroughly. In a small saucepan heat the butter, honey, the remaining 1 teaspoon salt, black pepper, and lemon juice. Pour the butter mixture over the hot carrots. Toss with the walnuts.

Makes 8 servings.

Ritzy Chicken

This chicken is easy, yet so good.

2	cups butter cracker crumbs
1	cup grated Parmesan cheese
⅓	cup fresh parsley
2	teaspoons salt
¼	teaspoon black pepper
1	cup butter, melted
10	(5-ounce) boneless, skinless chicken breasts

Preheat the oven to 350 degrees. Line a 15 x 10-inch baking pan with aluminum foil. Butter the foil. In a shallow dish mix the cracker crumbs, Parmesan cheese, parsley, salt, and pepper. In another shallow dish place the melted butter. Dip each chicken piece in the butter and then roll in the crumb mixture. Arrange in the prepared pan and bake uncovered for 45 minutes.

Makes 10 servings.

Corn Cheese Pudding

 2 tablespoons flour
 2 tablespoons sugar
 2 tablespoons butter, melted
 ½ cup milk
 1 cup shredded cheddar cheese
 2 large eggs, slightly beaten
 2 cups frozen cream-style corn, thawed
 1 teaspoon salt

Preheat the oven to 350 degrees. Grease a 2-quart baking dish. In a medium bowl combine the flour, sugar, and melted butter. Add the milk, cheese, and eggs, mixing well. Add the corn and salt, mixing well. Pour the mixture into the prepared casserole dish. Bake for approximately 45 minutes or until firm to the touch.

Makes 6 servings.

Hot Chicken Salad with Potato Chip Topping

While you don't usually think of chicken salad as a main dish, this one definitely is. Serve it alongside a salad and a vegetable and you have a delicious dinner.

4	cups diced, cooked chicken
½	cup finely chopped celery
2	teaspoons minced onion
1	tablespoon lemon juice
1	teaspoon salt
¾	cup slivered almonds
1	cup mayonnaise
1	(10.75-ounce) can cream of chicken soup
1	cup shredded cheddar cheese
2	cups crushed potato chips (plain or ruffled)

Preheat the oven to 350 degrees. Grease a 13 x 9-inch baking dish. In a large bowl combine the chicken, celery, onion, lemon juice, salt, almonds, mayonnaise, soup, and cheddar cheese. Mix well and place in the prepared dish. Top with the crushed potato chips. Bake for 25 minutes or until hot and bubbly.

Makes 8 servings.

NOTE: Cover loosely with foil if the potato chips begin to brown.

Apple Peanut Salad

Serve this in your prettiest dish. While this is a delicious salad, it isn't the most colorful.

- 1 (20-ounce) can crushed pineapple
- 1 ½ tablespoons apple cider vinegar
- 1 large egg, beaten
- 1 tablespoon all-purpose flour
- ½ cup sugar
- 2 cups miniature marshmallows
- 5 medium Granny Smith apples, peeled and diced right before serving
- 1 (12-ounce) carton frozen whipped topping, thawed
- 1 ½ cups salted peanuts, coarsely chopped

In a medium saucepan drain the pineapple juice and set the pineapple aside. Add the vinegar, egg, flour, and sugar to the pineapple juice and cook over medium heat, stirring constantly until thick. Let the mixture cool for 30 minutes and then add the crushed pineapple and marshmallows. Refrigerate overnight.

Right before you're ready to serve, peel and dice the apples. If you do this step too soon your apples will turn brown. Add the diced apples, whipped topping, and peanuts to the refrigerated mixture. Mix well and serve.

Makes 10 servings.

Pork Tenderloin with Mustard Corn Bread Crust

Quick, easy, and delicious! Isn't that what we want our food to be?

1	(1- to 1 ½-pound) pork tenderloin
2	teaspoons salt
1	teaspoon black pepper
1	tablespoon olive oil
1	tablespoon butter
1	teaspoon minced garlic
1 ½	cups crumbled corn bread
2	tablespoons Dijon mustard

Preheat the oven to 400 degrees. Grease a 13 x 9-inch baking pan and set aside. Trim the silver skin on the tenderloin and sprinkle with the salt and pepper. In a 9-inch skillet over high heat, add the olive oil and butter and sear the pork on all sides, turning frequently to brown. Place the tenderloin in the prepared pan, reserving the pan drippings. Add the garlic to the drippings and sauté for 30 seconds. Remove from the heat and add the crumbled corn bread. Coat the surface of the pork with the Dijon mustard. Pat the crumb mixture over the pork.

Roast for 25 to 30 minutes or until a thermometer inserted into the pork registers 160 degrees. Cover loosely with foil if it begins to get too brown. Remove from the oven and let the meat rest 15 minutes before slicing.

Makes 4 servings.

Double Chocolate Pound Cake

Moist and good and chocolaty! Need I say more?

1	cup butter
2	cups sugar
4	large eggs
⅔	cup chocolate syrup
2 ½	cups sifted all-purpose flour
¼	teaspoon salt
1	cup buttermilk
½	teaspoon baking soda
7	ounces milk chocolate bars
1	teaspoon vanilla extract

Preheat the oven to 350 degrees. Grease and flour one 10-inch tube cake pan. In a large bowl cream the butter and sugar. Add the eggs one at a time, beating after each addition. Add the chocolate syrup, flour, and salt. In a small bowl combine the buttermilk and baking soda and add to the flour mixture. In a double boiler melt the chocolate bars. Add the melted chocolate and vanilla to the batter. Pour the batter into the prepared pan and bake for 1 hour and 10 minutes or until a toothpick inserted in the center of the pan comes out clean.

Cool for 10 minutes before turning out onto a cake plate.

Makes 16 servings.

Chocolate Cobbler

I wish I was as rich as this dessert.

½	cup butter
1 ½	cups self-rising flour
2 ¾	cups sugar, divided
1 ¾	tablespoons plus ⅓ cup cocoa, divided
¾	cup milk
1	teaspoon vanilla extract
2 ¼	cups boiling water
	Vanilla ice cream

Preheat the oven to 350 degrees. Place the butter in a 13 x 9-inch baking dish and put it in the oven for 3 to 4 minutes to melt.

Meanwhile, in a medium bowl combine the flour, 1 ¼ cups of the sugar, 1 ¾ tablespoons of the cocoa, the milk, and the vanilla. Stir until well blended. Drop the batter by spoonfuls onto the melted butter. In a separate bowl, combine the remaining 1 ½ cups sugar and the remaining ⅓ cup cocoa. Sprinkle the cocoa mixture over the batter. Pour the boiling water over the batter. Do not stir. Bake for 40 to 45 minutes. Let stand 15 minutes before serving.

Serve with vanilla ice cream.

Makes 10 to 12 servings.

Raspberry Cream Cheese Pie

I love the combination of chocolate and raspberries.

Crust:
1 ½ cups chocolate wafer crumbs
2 tablespoons sugar
⅓ cup melted butter

Filling:
4 ounces cream cheese, softened
1 (14-ounce) can sweetened condensed milk
3 tablespoons lemon juice
1 teaspoon vanilla extract
1 large egg, slightly beaten
1 cup fresh raspberries

Chocolate glaze:
¼ cup semisweet chocolate chips
¼ cup heavy cream

To make the crust: Preheat the oven to 350 degrees. Lightly grease a 9-inch pie pan. Combine the wafer crumbs, sugar, and butter. Press the mixture on the bottom and up the sides of the pie pan. Bake for 10 minutes. Cool 30 minutes before adding the filling.

To make the filling: In a medium bowl combine the cream cheese, condensed milk, lemon juice, vanilla, and egg. Set aside. Layer the raspberries on top of the cooled crust. Pour the cream cheese mixture over the raspberries. Bake for 30 minutes.

To make the chocolate glaze: In a small saucepan place the chocolate chips and heavy cream over low heat, stirring constantly until the chips are melted. After you remove the pie from the oven, drizzle the glaze over the top. Refrigerate for at least 4 hours before serving.

Makes 1 pie or 6 to 8 servings.

♥ CHAPTER 3 ♥

TENDING THE SICK

FOOD FOR WHAT AILS YOU

Whether it's for a young neighbor who's having a difficult pregnancy or an elderly church member who broke his hip, food is a tangible way we can express our concern for another human being. While homemade macaroni and cheese can't replace medicine, it can go a long way toward lifting someone's spirits. At the very least, food from a friend allows the recipient to rest instead of worry about grocery shopping and cooking. And Southerners seem to have a sixth sense for knowing when it's time to come calling.

♥

Cora Lynn learned the hard way that canned vegetables don't count. Her mother was out of town, so she had to fill in at the last minute to prepare a meal for the widow Olivia, the longtime piano teacher who was suffering from yet another bout of an undiagnosable malaise.

Turns out Cora Lynn's mother forgot she had volunteered to take dinner on Tuesday and so she called Cora Lynn, frantic, from a sauna in Hot Springs where she had gone for a "girls' getaway" with her roommates from college. Cora Lynn had no idea why those women thought they could get away with referring to themselves as "girls" now that every last one of them was past forty. But her mother promised her a gift certificate for her trouble, so Cora Lynn flipped through the small black three-ring binder that her mother kept on the kitchen counter, the one with recipes from dead relatives, and got to work.

She had seen her mother do this many times, prepare a casserole or a pot of soup to take to someone who was sick. Neighbors, church members, and once even the recording secretary from DAR, a woman her mother claimed to loathe.

So Cora Lynn knew about defrosting the chicken and preheating the oven. She even remembered to squeeze excess water from the spinach. When the timer went off, she had a piece of aluminum foil at the ready. She was halfway out the door before she wondered if she was supposed to take anything else to Miss Olivia. Did her mother usually include a vegetable or a salad? Unsure of what to do, she grabbed a can of asparagus spears from the pantry and stuck it in her purse. Her father was always complimenting her on her resourceful nature, so it was with confidence that she rang Miss Olivia's doorbell—twice, because Miss Olivia didn't like wearing her hearing aids.

Cora Lynn thought maybe Miss Olivia had developed a problem with her throat, in addition to her other various maladies, because she was speechless as Cora Lynn placed the chicken divan on the kitchen table and pulled out the can of asparagus spears from her purse. She thought it a little rude that Miss Olivia didn't walk her back to the front door, but she knew the old lady wasn't feeling well so she decided not to mention it. One of her mother's favorite sayings was, "Don't say anything if it can't be nice," so Cora Lynn let herself out.

Even though Miss Olivia didn't move around as quickly as she used to, what with her overall poor health and the undue stress from all the trouble she's seen during her lifetime—"more than most people could bear"—after Cora Lynn left Miss Olivia couldn't get to the phone fast enough to spread the word of the canned vegetable masquerading as concern.

Cora Lynn thought it was enough that she had prepared the chicken divan according to her mother's recipe and called to schedule a convenient time to drop it by. But Cora Lynn was young, and she didn't realize she'd violated one of the cardinal rules of culinary caregiving. Her mother set her straight the minute she got back from Hot Springs.

"You always take a complete meal," said her mother. "If you're part of a group effort, then each person signs up for one food item, such as salad or dessert. But if you're thoughtful enough to assume responsibility all on your own, you need to take more than just the main dish. It's preferable that everything be homemade. People aren't usually too demanding about the bread, though; they realize you'll probably stop by the bakery on the way over. But under no circumstances do you offer a can of anything to an ailing person and expect it to make them feel better."

Before Cora Lynn could say she thought this was entirely too complicated, her mother whispered that if she ever found herself in such a pickle again she could resort to a canned vegetable only if she took the time to put the contents in a dish. She also told Cora Lynn not to ever utter a word about that particular little trick. In the end, though, it was just one of many secrets the two would share in that kitchen, thereby securing the sanctity of their mother-daughter bond for years to come.

Southern Pecan Pie Muffins

When you deliver these muffins, save yourself some time and print out the recipe and take it along—people always ask for it.

    4 large eggs
    1 cup butter, softened
    2 cups firmly packed brown sugar
    1 cup all-purpose flour
    2 cups chopped pecans

Preheat the oven to 350 degrees. Prepare two 12-cup muffin tins with nonstick cooking spray or paper muffin liners. Beat the eggs until fluffy, add the butter, and continue to mix. Add the brown sugar and flour and mix until the ingredients are just moistened. Fold in the pecans. Spoon the batter evenly into the muffin cups until each is ⅔ full. Bake for 20 minutes. Cool for 10 minutes before removing from muffin cups.

Makes 24 muffins.

Baked Green Peas with Pearl Onions

This looks as good when it comes out of the oven as it did when you prepared it. You can't say that about too many dishes.

    1 (16-ounce) bag frozen green peas
    1 (8-ounce) package button mushrooms
    4 ounces frozen pearl onions
    ½ teaspoon salt
    ¼ teaspoon black pepper
    1 tablespoon olive oil
    3 tablespoons melted butter

Preheat the oven to 400 degrees. In a 13 x 9-inch baking dish add the peas, mushrooms, onions, salt, and pepper. Drizzle with the olive oil and melted butter. Bake for 20 minutes, stirring occasionally.

Makes 6 servings.

Peachy Keen Salad

The South is known for its fresh peaches. It's a shame that the time we get them is so limited. This recipe is just one way you can enjoy peaches all year long.

        1   (20-ounce) can sliced peaches
        2   (3-ounce) packages peach gelatin
    1 ½   cups buttermilk
        1   (8-ounce) carton frozen whipped topping, thawed

In a medium saucepan mash the sliced peaches with a potato masher. Heat mashed peaches over medium heat. Add the gelatin and stir until dissolved. Cool for 30 minutes. Add the buttermilk, stir well, and refrigerate the mixture for 1 hour or until the mixture begins to jell. Fold in the whipped topping. Pour into a 13 x 9-inch dish. Refrigerate for 4 hours before serving.

Makes 10 servings.

Pimento and Cheese, Cheese, Cheese

This isn't your everyday pimento and cheese recipe. The three cheeses and the two kinds of pepper make this a burst of flavor in the mouth.

        2   cups shredded cheddar cheese
        1   cup shredded Monterey Jack cheese
        ½   cup grated Parmesan cheese
        1   (7-ounce) jar diced pimentos, drained
        1   to 1 ½ cups mayonnaise
        ½   teaspoon salt
        ½   teaspoon black pepper,
        ⅛   teaspoon cayenne pepper

In a large mixing bowl combine the cheddar, Monterey Jack, and Parmesan cheeses. Add the diced pimientos, mayonnaise, salt, black pepper, and cayenne pepper. Stir to mix well. Cover and place in the refrigerator.

Makes 4 cups.

NOTE: Use as a sandwich filling, with crackers, or stuffed in celery sticks.

Corn Chowder

I serve this year round. But I have to admit this is especially good in the summertime when the corn is fresh from the garden.

- 4 slices bacon, diced
- ½ cup finely diced onion
- 1 teaspoon minced garlic
- ¼ teaspoon cayenne pepper
- 3 cups peeled and diced baking potatoes
- 4 cups fresh or frozen whole kernel corn
- 8 cups (64 ounces) chicken broth, canned or homemade
- 1 cup milk
- 1 cup heavy cream
- ½ teaspoon salt
- ½ teaspoon black pepper

In a 6-quart stockpot or Dutch oven, add the diced bacon and cook over medium heat until browned. Add the onions and cook until translucent. Add the garlic, cayenne pepper, potatoes, corn, and chicken broth. Bring to a boil, stirring to combine the ingredients. Reduce the heat and simmer, stirring occasionally until the potatoes are tender. This should take about 15 to 20 minutes. Add the milk, cream, salt, and pepper and mix well. Heat through, being careful not to allow the soup to boil. Serve warm.

Makes 6 to 8 servings.

Chicken Dumplin' Soup

In this recipe we take the south-of-the-border tortilla and turn it into a traditional Southern dumplin'. And the good thing is that no one will ever know the difference.

8	cups (64 ounces) chicken broth, canned or homemade
½	cup finely chopped onion
1	cup finely chopped carrots
1	cup finely chopped celery
3	(7-inch) flour tortillas cut into ½- x 2-inch strips
1	(4-ounce) can sliced mushrooms, drained
2	to 3 cups cooked and chopped chicken
½	teaspoon salt
½	teaspoon black pepper
¼	cup toasted slivered almonds
1	cup heavy cream
2	tablespoons chopped parsley (optional)

In a 6-quart stockpot combine the chicken broth, onion, carrots, celery, and tortillas. Bring to a boil and then reduce the heat to simmer and cook uncovered for 20 minutes. Add the mushrooms, chicken, salt, and pepper and continue to simmer for an additional 10 minutes. Add the almonds and heavy cream. Heat just to serving temperature. Garnish with chopped parsley, if desired.

Makes 8 servings.

Sausage and Egg Casserole

Quick and easy! You can prepare this a day ahead so that you can put it in the oven as you start your day. This casserole and some fresh fruit make a perfect Southern breakfast.

8	large eggs, boiled, peeled, and sliced
½	teaspoon salt
½	teaspoon black pepper
1	pound hot or mild pork sausage, cooked and drained
1 ½	cups sour cream
¾	cup dry bread crumbs
1 ½	cups grated cheddar cheese

Preheat the oven to 400 degrees. Grease a 13 x 9-inch baking dish. Place the eggs in the baking dish and sprinkle with the salt and pepper. Add the sausage on top of the eggs. Spread the sour cream over the sausage. In a small mixing bowl mix the bread crumbs and cheese. Sprinkle the cheese mixture over the sour cream. Place in the oven for about 15 minutes to heat thoroughly, until lightly browned.

Makes 8 to 10 servings.

Apricot Sweet and Sour Tea

This is one of the prettiest beverages I serve, and I believe it helps people feel better as they enjoy it.

6	(individual-size) tea bags
4	cups boiling water
½	cup sugar
2	(11.3 ounce) cans apricot nectar
1	(12-ounce) can lemonade concentrate, thawed
2	(12-ounce) cans ginger ale

Place the tea bags in a gallon pitcher, pour the boiling water over them, and let the tea steep for 5 minutes. Remove the tea bags, add the sugar, and stir until dissolved. Add the apricot nectar, lemonade concentrate, and ginger ale and stir until well mixed. Serve over ice.

Makes 12 servings.

NOTE: Keep refrigerated.

Potato and Cheese Soup

This soup always makes me feel better.

8 medium baking potatoes, peeled and chopped (3 pounds)
1 cup finely chopped carrots
1 cup finely chopped celery
½ cup finely chopped onion
4 cups (32 ounces) chicken broth, canned or homemade
3 cups half-and-half
1 teaspoon salt
½ teaspoon black pepper
2 cups cubed Velveeta cheese

In a large Dutch oven, cook the potatoes, carrots, celery, and onion in the chicken broth over medium heat for 15 to 20 minutes or until tender. Stir in the half-and-half, salt, and pepper. Cook and stir until heated thoroughly. Add the cheese and stir until melted.

Makes 8 servings.

Brown Rice Casserole with Pecans

This is a very nice complement to any beef dish. Try it with beef stroganoff. If you want to use this with a chicken dish, just substitute a can of chicken broth for the beef consommé.

4 tablespoons butter
½ cup finely chopped onion
½ cup finely chopped celery
1 cup brown rice, uncooked
1 cup pecans, chopped
1 (10 ¾-ounce) can beef consommé or broth
10 ¾ ounces water

Preheat the oven to 350 degrees. Grease a 2-quart baking dish. In a medium saucepan melt the butter over low heat. Add the onion and celery. Sauté for 3 to 4 minutes. Add the rice and pecans and cook 2 minutes longer. Spoon the mixture into the prepared dish. Pour the consommé and water over the top and stir to mix. Cover and bake for 1 hour.

Makes 6 to 8 servings.

Cheese Biscuits

This is a great biscuit to serve with country ham.

- 2 cups all-purpose flour
- 1 teaspoon salt
- 4 teaspoons baking powder
- ⅓ cup vegetable shortening
- 1 cup grated sharp cheddar cheese
- ¼ cup Parmesan cheese
- ¼ teaspoon crushed red pepper
- 1 cup milk

Preheat the oven to 400 degrees. Grease a 13 x 9-inch baking pan. In a large bowl sift the flour, salt, and baking powder. Cut in the shortening until the mixture resembles small peas. Mix in the cheddar cheese, Parmesan cheese, and red pepper. Add the milk, stirring well to make a soft dough. Knead slightly. Roll the dough to ½-inch thickness. Cut into biscuit shapes. Bake for 10 to 12 minutes.

Makes 16 to 18 biscuits.

Bacon and Cheese Layered Red Potatoes

This recipe epitomizes the term "comfort food." And isn't that what we are really trying to do when we take a covered dish to someone who isn't feeling well—comfort them?

- 12 to 14 medium-size red potatoes
- 2 cups shredded cheddar cheese
- 12 slices bacon, cooked and crumbled
- 1 teaspoon salt
- ½ teaspoon black pepper
- ½ cup butter, melted

Preheat the oven to 350 degrees. Grease a 13 x 9-inch baking dish and set aside. Wash the potatoes. Slice unpeeled potatoes into ¼-inch-thick slices and place in a large saucepan. Add water until the potatoes are covered by 1 inch. Place a lid on the saucepan and cook over medium heat for about 15 to 20 minutes or until tender. Drain and place ½ the potatoes, cheese, bacon, salt, and pepper in the prepared baking dish. Repeat to form a second layer. Pour the melted butter over the top. Place in the oven and bake for 15 minutes or until the cheese melts.

Makes 10 to 12 servings.

Water Tower Chicken with Two Cheeses

Our home is next to the water tower where I live in Charlotte, Tennessee. In such a small town, it is a landmark. That's how I feel about this recipe. It's one of my favorites and one I have served in my home, right next to the water tower, for years and years.

2	large eggs, well beaten
1	cup milk
6	(5-ounce) chicken breasts, cut into bite-size pieces
1 ½	cups dry seasoned Italian bread crumbs
¾	cup butter, divided
1	(8-ounce) package sliced fresh mushrooms
1 ½	cups shredded cheddar cheese
1 ½	cups shredded mozzarella cheese
2	cups chicken broth

In a large bowl beat the eggs and milk together. Add the chicken to the milk mixture. Cover and refrigerate for 6 hours. Drain the chicken and discard the milk mixture. Place the bread crumbs in a shallow dish and roll the chicken pieces in the bread crumbs until coated.

In a large skillet over medium heat melt ¼ cup of the butter. When the butter is hot, sauté ½ of the chicken pieces over medium heat until they are cooked, turning frequently for about 10 minutes. Remove and drain on a paper towel. Add another ¼ cup of the butter and cook the rest of the chicken. Add the remaining ¼ cup butter and sauté the mushrooms for five minutes.

Preheat the oven to 350 degrees. Grease a 3-quart casserole dish. Layer ½ of the chicken, ½ of the cheddar and mozzarella cheese, and ½ of the mushrooms. Repeat to make a second layer. Pour the chicken broth over the top. Bake uncovered for 25 minutes, until heated thoroughly.

Makes 6 to 8 servings.

Ham and Cheese Quiche

One reason I like taking this to someone is that they can eat it at any time of the day. And it is so easy to reheat.

1	tablespoon butter
2	tablespoons minced onion
½	cup diced ham
1	(9-inch) deep dish unbaked piecrust
1	cup grated Swiss cheese
3	large eggs
1 ½	cups milk
½	teaspoon salt
½	teaspoon black pepper

Preheat the oven to 350 degrees. Melt the butter in a small saucepan. Add the onion and cook for 3 minutes or until soft. Add the ham and continue to cook for 1 minute. Sprinkle the onion and ham evenly over the piecrust. Sprinkle the cheese over the onion and ham. In a small bowl whisk the eggs and milk together until well combined. Add the salt and pepper. Pour the egg mixture into the piecrust. Bake for 30 minutes or until the middle is firm to the touch.

Makes 6 to 8 servings.

Beef Stroganoff

While this is a great comfort food for a sick friend, it is also good enough to serve the preacher for Sunday dinner. And that's high praise.

2 tablespoons oil

2 pounds sirloin steak, cut into 1 ½-inch cubes

2 tablespoons butter

2 tablespoons flour

1 (10 ¾-ounce) can cream of mushroom soup

1 (3-ounce) can sliced mushrooms, drained

1 (10 ¾-ounce) can beef broth

1 teaspoon garlic salt

1 cup sour cream (optional)

Preheat the oven to 350 degrees. In a large skillet heat the oil over medium heat. Brown the meat in small batches and set aside. In the same skillet add the butter, flour, cream of mushroom soup, sliced mushrooms, beef broth, and garlic salt, stirring well to combine all the ingredients. Add the meat to the skillet. Cover and place the skillet in the oven. Continue to cook for 1 ½ hours or until the meat is tender. Remove from the oven and add sour cream if desired. Return the skillet to the oven for 5 minutes. Serve over rice or noodles.

Makes 8 servings.

Judith Diehl's Aggression Cookies

I hope everyone is as lucky as I am to have had a friend like Judith Diehl. We shared so many good times together, and she always served these cookies. I miss her.

1 ½   cups butter, softened
1 ½   cups firmly packed brown sugar
  3   cups quick-cooking oats
1 ½   cups all-purpose flour
1 ½   teaspoons baking soda

Preheat the oven to 350 degrees. Lightly grease a large cookie sheet. In a large bowl combine the softened butter, brown sugar, and oats. In a small bowl mix the flour and baking soda together. Add this to the oat mixture and use your hands to form a dough. Shape the dough into small balls. Place on the prepared cookie sheet two 2 inches apart and flatten with a fork. Bake each batch for 8 to 10 minutes. Remove from the cookie sheet and cool on a wire rack. Makes 4 to 5 dozen cookies.

Caramel Banana Pie

Many of the South's best restaurants have been serving this pie for decades. Not everyone can make caramel the old-fashioned way in a cast-iron skillet without burning it. But everyone can make it with this method. Just make sure that you keep the cans covered with water the entire time.

2   (14-ounce) cans sweetened condensed milk
2   medium-size bananas
1   (9-inch) graham cracker crust
1   cup heavy cream
¼   chopped and toasted pecans

Remove the labels from the cans of condensed milk. Place in a large stockpot. Cover with water by 4 inches. Place over medium heat and bring the water to a boil. Reduce the heat to low and simmer for 3 hours. Keep the cans covered with water at all times. Remove from the heat and let cool. When cool, open with can opener. The mixture will be caramel. Slice the bananas into the piecrust and pour the caramel filling over the top. Whip the heavy cream with an electric mixer until soft peaks form. Place the whipped cream topping over the caramel filling and garnish with pecans. Makes 1 pie or 10 servings.

Cherry Pie

This is my favorite pie in the book. I have been using this recipe for more than thirty years. It really is a good one.

Double piecrust:
2   cups all-purpose flour
1   teaspoon salt
⅔   cup vegetable shortening
7   to 8 tablespoons cold water

Filling:
2   (14.5-ounce) cans pitted tart red cherries
1   cup sugar
¼   cup firmly packed brown sugar
4   tablespoons cornstarch
⅛   teaspoon salt
2   tablespoons butter
¼   teaspoon almond extract
¼   teaspoon red food coloring

To make the double crust: Sift together the flour and salt. Cut in the shortening until the pieces are the size of small peas. Sprinkle the water over the dry ingredients one tablespoon at a time, stirring to incorporate. When all the dry ingredients are moistened, form the dough into a ball and refrigerate for 30 minutes. Divide dough into two parts. Roll each into a 10-inch circle. In a 9-inch pie pan place one of the piecrusts.

To make the filling: Preheat the oven to 375 degrees. Drain the cherries and reserve 1 cup of the liquid. In a 2-quart saucepan combine the reserved cherry juice, sugar, brown sugar, cornstarch, and salt. Bring to a boil over medium heat and stir until thickened. Remove from the heat and add the cherries, butter, almond extract, and food coloring.

To assemble the pie: Place the filling into the pie pan lined with the crust. Take the other piecrust and cut ½-inch-wide strips, placing crisscross across the pie to form a lattice topping. Bake for 45 to 50 minutes or until golden brown.

Makes 1 pie or 6 to 8 servings.

NOTE: You can use store-bought crusts for any of the pies in this book, but I hope you will try to make this piecrust.

♥ CHAPTER 4 ♥

FAMILY REUNIONS

BLOOD IS THICKER
THAN MOLASSES

Having the family reunion catered would be a disaster, and Cousin Mercy came right out and said so the minute her harebrained sister Augusta suggested it.

"That will be a disaster," said Cousin Mercy, who knew that half the fun of a family reunion is preparing your favorite dishes for sharing and showing off. But Augusta was stubborn, always had been. After last year, when a handful of cousins got sick at the last minute and couldn't bring the meats they had signed up to provide and everyone ended up eating extra helpings of crunchy coleslaw and three-bean salad to get full, Augusta vowed that things were going to change when it was her turn to organize the reunion.

The minute their family members started calling to ask what they should bring to the reunion, Cousin Mercy was not surprised at their reactions when she repeated what Augusta had told her to say: "There will be a Mason jar on each picnic table for you to contribute whatever money you feel is fair toward the enjoyment and sustainment of your extended family. So just bring yourselves. And your wallets." Cousin Mercy was pretty sure *sustenance* was the word Augusta was looking for, but, again, you can't tell her sister anything once she sets her mind in a certain direction.

♥

The Watsons had long outgrown being able to have their annual family gathering in a relative's home. After the twins were born, it seemed every year or two another set of multiples arrived until there was no more room at the inn, so to speak. For a few years they met at the high school gymnasium. But then the principal upped the fee when other families started calling to rent the space and he realized there was money to be made. To prove she was nobody's fool, Augusta went to the chamber of commerce and researched more economical options. She settled on a state park that promised "a tranquil setting for gatherings of all kinds."

For years, Granddaddy Samuel had been wishing for just such a location so he and Uncle Seth and the boys could schedule a comeback appearance for their band. They hadn't been allowed to play since the unfortunate incident of 2003. But if they were going to be out in the woods, surely Augusta would have to say yes.

Cousin Mercy thought moving the reunion was enough change for one year, but Augusta had her mind set on hiring her friend from the beauty shop who "caters." Cousin Mercy had her suspicions about whether the hairstylist could really pull this off—feeding Watsons of varying ages and food preferences from three states—because all she's ever known the woman to cook is spaghetti for the Humane Society's fund-raising supper every spring. It tastes fine, Cousin Mercy admits, but nothing to write home about. Nothing like her own mother can make when you sweet-talk her long enough. But Mama had stopped taking food of any kind to the reunions after that time she overheard someone accuse her of using canned peaches in her cobbler.

"That woman couldn't tell a fresh peach from a stale rutabaga," Mama had said. Mama never would reveal who had insulted her, but we're pretty sure it was her brother's third wife, the one who went on and on about the time she got her letter to the editor printed in the paper when the town council threatened to install parking meters around the town square. You didn't dare ask her even to pass the Tabasco for fear she'd talk your ears off about that letter.

♥

So no one really knew what to expect this year. If they were lucky, the food would be good and no one would complain too much about having to put money in the kitty. Hopefully Uncle Mack wouldn't make a fool out of himself, or cause bodily injury, trying to beat the kids at horseshoes. Last summer at the Fourth of July picnic at the lake, he sent the u-shaped piece of iron sailing smack into Brother Joshua's new truck. Him being a man of God and all, Brother Joshua didn't cuss or anything, but you could tell he was peeved.

As the day for the reunion drew closer, Cousin Mercy has to admit she was worried. She had her doubts. But she tried to hang on to what she knew to be true in her heart of hearts: her family always comes through for one another, even if they sometimes butt heads along the way. She suspected that most of them would bring fried chicken or potato salad or, at the very least, a dozen cheese biscuits, whether they had been asked to bring food or not. The cousins who dropped the ball on the meat for last year's reunion might very well show up with a whole roasted pig to make amends. For like their ancestors before them, Watsons simply don't feel right about leaving the house empty-handed. It's just the kind of people they are.

Sweet Tea

The one and only official drink of the South!

- 4 cups water plus additional water to fill a gallon container
- 8 small (individual size) tea bags
- 2 cups sugar

Bring the water to a boil in a medium saucepan. Add the tea bags and sugar and remove from the heat. Let the tea steep for 20 minutes. Remove and discard the tea bags and pour the tea into a gallon container. Add enough water to make a gallon and cool in the refrigerator. Serve over ice.

Makes 8 to 10 servings.

Bread and Butter Pickles

These are great on sandwiches, but I have even seen people take a spoonful and eat them as a vegetable.

- 1 gallon medium cucumbers
- 6 medium white onions, sliced
- 3 cloves garlic
- ⅓ cup kosher salt
- 5 pounds crushed ice
- 5 cups sugar
- 3 cups apple cider vinegar
- 1 ½ teaspoons turmeric
- 1 ½ teaspoons celery seed
- 2 tablespoons mustard seed

Thinly slice the cucumbers and place in a large nonreactive bowl. Add the onions, garlic cloves, and salt. Cover with the crushed ice. Mix thoroughly. Let stand 3 hours and drain well. Place the cucumber mixture in a large stainless steel stockpot. In a large bowl combine the sugar, vinegar, turmeric, celery seed, and mustard seed. Pour the mixture over the cucumbers and bring to a boil, boiling for 2 minutes. Pack into 8 sterilized pint jars.

Makes 8 pints.

Deep Fried Corn Bread

    Vegetable oil for frying
 1 cup self-rising white cornmeal
 ½ cup all-purpose flour
 2 teaspoons baking powder
 ½ teaspoon salt
 ½ cup finely chopped onion
 1 large egg, slightly beaten
 1 (10-ounce) can diced tomatoes and green chilies, partially drained

In a large skillet or deep fryer, heat the oil to 350 degrees. In a large bowl combine the cornmeal, flour, baking powder, and salt. Add the onion, egg, and the diced tomatoes and green chilies, stirring to mix well. Drop by teaspoonfuls into the hot oil. Fry until golden brown, turning as needed. Drain on a paper towel.

Makes 6 to 8 servings.

Scalloped Potatoes with Country Ham

The country ham flavor combined with the cheese and cream makes this dish really special.

 6 medium potatoes, peeled and thinly sliced
 ½ cup diced country ham
 2 tablespoons finely diced onion
 1 teaspoon minced garlic
 2 cups heavy cream
 1 cup grated cheddar cheese
 1 teaspoon salt
 ¼ teaspoon cayenne pepper

Preheat the oven to 350 degrees. Grease a 13 x 9-inch baking dish and set aside. In a large bowl combine the potatoes, ham, onion, garlic, cream, cheese, salt, and cayenne pepper, and stir to coat the potatoes. Spread the potato mixture evenly in the prepared baking dish. Cover with aluminum foil and bake for 1 ½ hours or until the potatoes are tender. Remove the foil and continue baking for 15 minutes to brown the top.

Makes 8 servings.

Baked Bean Casserole

Thanks to my friend Donna Stock for this delicious recipe.

1	(29-ounce) can pork and beans
1	(15-ounce) can kidney beans, drained
1	(15-ounce) can lima beans, drained
1	(15-ounce) can whole kernel corn, drained
1	pound hamburger meat
½	cup finely chopped onion
½	cup finely chopped green bell pepper
¼	cup firmly packed brown sugar
½	cup ketchup
2	tablespoons apple cider vinegar
1	tablespoon mustard
½	teaspoon salt
1	teaspoon black pepper
8	slices bacon, uncooked

Preheat the oven to 300 degrees. Grease a 13 x 9-inch baking dish. Set aside. In a large mixing bowl combine the pork and beans, kidney beans, lima beans, and corn and set aside. In a large skillet brown the hamburger meat over medium heat, stirring to crumble. Add the onion and bell pepper and continue to stir until soft. Drain the grease. Add the brown sugar, ketchup, vinegar, mustard, salt, and pepper to the skillet and stir well. Pour the hamburger mixture in the bowl with beans and corn and stir to mix. Place in the prepared baking dish. Top with the bacon slices. Bake uncovered for 1 ½ hours.

Makes 16 servings.

Corn and Black Bean Salad

I love to make this during the summer months. It is great to serve at an outdoor family reunion.

Dressing:
- ½ cup apple cider vinegar
- ¼ cup sugar
- ½ teaspoon salt
- ½ teaspoon black pepper

Salad:
- 1 (15-ounce) can white whole kernel corn, drained
- 1 (15-ounce) can yellow whole kernel corn, drained
- 1 (15-ounce) can black beans, drained and rinsed
- ½ cup diced red bell pepper
- 1 cup diced green bell pepper
- 1 cup diced purple onion
- 2 cups diced (fresh) tomatoes
- 1 medium cucumber, peeled, seeded, and diced

To make the dressing: In a small bowl whisk the vinegar, sugar, salt, and pepper until the sugar dissolves.

To make the salad: In a large bowl combine the corns, black beans, red and green pepper, onion, tomato, and cucumber. Toss to mix. Add the dressing to the salad. Cover and chill 4 hours before serving.

Makes 10 servings.

Frozen Peach Salad

This is your basic traditional Southern frozen salad. Good enough to eat as a dessert, but why deprive yourself of dessert? Eat this with your meal as a side dish.

- 1 (20-ounce) can peach pie filling
- 1 (20-ounce) can crushed pineapple, drained
- 1 (12-ounce) carton frozen whipped topping, thawed
- 1 (14-ounce) can sweetened condensed milk

In a large bowl combine the pie filling, drained pineapple, whipped topping, and condensed milk. Pour into a 13 x 9-inch glass dish. Freeze overnight.

Makes 12 servings.

Chicken Breasts Stuffed with Ham and Cheese

This is my son's favorite and I make it for him every year on his birthday.

6	large boneless, skinless chicken breast halves
1	teaspoon salt
6	thin slices deli ham
1	(8-ounce) block Swiss cheese, cut into 6 pieces
½	cup all-purpose flour
¼	cup butter
½	cup water
1	chicken bouillon cube
1	(3-ounce) can sliced mushrooms, drained
⅓	cup white wine (or chicken broth)
½	cup slivered almonds, toasted

Gravy:

2	tablespoons all-purpose flour
½	cup water
	Reserved pan drippings

Preheat the oven to 350 degrees. Grease a 13 x 9-inch baking dish and set aside. Cover the chicken breasts with plastic wrap and pound to flatten into ¼-inch thickness. Remove the plastic wrap and sprinkle the chicken breasts with salt. Arrange the ham and cheese slices on each piece of chicken. Roll up like a jellyroll. Secure with string or toothpicks if necessary. Place ½ cup flour in a shallow dish and roll each piece of chicken in the flour to coat.

In a large skillet melt the butter, add the chicken, and brown. Transfer the chicken to the prepared baking dish. Retain the pan drippings for the gravy. In the same skillet add the water, bouillon cube, mushrooms, and wine or broth, stirring well until the bouillon cube is dissolved. Pour over the chicken. Bake covered in aluminum foil for 1 hour. Arrange the chicken on a serving platter. Cover to keep warm. Remove strings or toothpicks if used.

To make the gravy: In a small saucepan blend the flour with the water and add the reserved pan drippings. Cook until thickened, stirring constantly.

To serve: Pour the gravy over the chicken. Garnish with the toasted almonds.

Makes 6 servings.

Carrot Fruit Salad

You know what they say about carrots being good for your eyes? Well this dish goes one step further—it is one of the most "eye-appealing" dishes I make.

- 6 cups grated carrots
- ½ cup golden raisins
- ½ cup crushed pineapple, drained
- ½ cup shredded coconut
- ⅓ cup mayonnaise
- 1 teaspoon sugar
- ⅛ teaspoon salt

In a serving bowl combine the carrots, raisins, pineapple, coconut, mayonnaise, sugar, and salt. Refrigerate until serving time.

Makes 6 to 8 servings.

NOTE: I like to prepare this at least 4 hours in advance. It can be made the day before serving.

Noodle Rice Casserole

This is wonderful served with beef.

- ½ cup butter
- 1 (4-ounce) package extra-fine noodles
- 1 cup regular uncooked long grain rice
- 1 ½ cups chicken broth, more if needed
- 1 (10.5-ounce) can French onion soup
- 2 tablespoons soy sauce
- ½ cup toasted almonds

Grease a 13 x 9-inch baking dish and set aside. Melt the butter in a large saucepan and sauté the raw noodles for 2 to 3 minutes or until just golden. Add the rice, chicken broth, French onion soup, and soy sauce. Cover and simmer for about 20 minutes, or until the rice is done. Add more broth if necessary to keep the rice moist. Preheat the oven to 325 degrees. Pour the noodle mixture into the prepared baking dish and sprinkle with the almonds. Bake uncovered for 30 minutes.

Makes 8 servings.

Macaroni and Cheese with Tomatoes

You will find several casserole dishes filled with traditional mac and cheese at any family reunion. This will make you the talk of the family—in a good way.

1 (8-ounce) box elbow macaroni
2 tablespoons vegetable oil
1 cup finely chopped onion
2 (10-ounce) cans diced tomatoes and green chilies
½ teaspoon salt
½ teaspoon black pepper
2 teaspoons Worcestershire sauce
4 cups grated cheddar cheese
1 cup butter cracker crumbs
¼ cup butter, thinly sliced

Preheat the oven to 375 degrees. Grease a 13 x 9-inch baking dish. Cook the macaroni according to package directions, drain and set aside. Place the oil in a 2-quart saucepan, add the onions and sauté for 2 minutes over medium heat. Add the tomatoes and green chilies, salt, pepper, and Worcestershire sauce. Cook for 20 minutes to reduce the liquid.

Place ½ the macaroni in the bottom of the prepared baking dish. Layer ½ the tomato mixture and cheese on top of the macaroni. Repeat each layer. Top with the cracker crumbs. Thinly slice the butter and place across the top. Bake for 20 to 25 minutes or until hot and bubbly and golden brown.

Makes 10 to 12 servings.

A Good Fruitcake

I am not the biggest fan of traditional fruitcake. But I love this variation.

- ½ pound candied cherries, diced
- ½ pound candied pineapple, diced
- 2 cups chopped pecans
- 1 pound chopped dates
- 1 (14-ounce) can sweetened condensed milk
- 1 (7-ounce) package flaked coconut
- ¼ teaspoon salt

Preheat the oven to 325 degrees. Line a 9 x 5 x 3-inch loaf pan with a brown paper bag cut to fit the pan. Grease and flour the paper. Set aside. In a large bowl mix the cherries, pineapple, pecans, dates, condensed milk, coconut, and salt, stirring to incorporate all the ingredients. Butter your hands and pack the mixture into the loaf pan. It is important to pack the mixture tightly, pressing down with the palms of your hands to accomplish this. Bake for 1 hour. Let cool in the pan. Remove from the pan and peel the paper from the cake. When completely cooled, wrap in plastic wrap and then in foil.

Makes 1 fruitcake or 24 servings.

NOTE: This will keep for up to four months and in the freezer for even longer.

Black Bean Soup

This is a good hearty soup.

2 (15-ounce) cans black beans, drained and rinsed
1 (15-ounce) can chopped tomatoes
1 (10-ounce) can tomatoes with green chilies
1 (15-ounce) can chicken broth
2 (4-ounce) cans green chilies
1 (15-ounce) can whole kernel corn
½ cup sliced green onions
2 tablespoons chili powder
2 teaspoons cumin

In a Dutch oven or large saucepan, combine the beans, chopped tomatoes, tomatoes with green chilies, chicken broth, green chilies, corn, green onions, chili powder, and cumin. Cook over medium heat until the mixture comes to a boil. Reduce the heat to simmer. Cover and simmer for 2 hours, stirring occasionally.

Makes 8 servings.

Fireman's Cabbage

I've got my brother Don to thank for this recipe. He was a newspaper photographer and picked up this recipe from a fire hall in Nashville where they cooked it up every week.

6   cups chopped cabbage (1 medium head of cabbage)
1   pound hot or mild pork sausage
½   cup finely chopped onion
½   cup finely chopped green bell pepper
1   teaspoon garlic salt
2   teaspoons chili powder
2   (15-ounce) cans diced tomatoes
1   teaspoon salt
½   teaspoon black pepper

Place the cabbage in a large saucepan with enough water to cover by 1 inch. Cook for 15 minutes over medium heat until just tender. Drain and set aside. In a large skillet brown the sausage, onion, and bell pepper. Add the garlic salt, chili powder, tomatoes, salt, and pepper and mix well. Add the sausage mixture to the cabbage and simmer for approximately 1 hour. Add additional salt and pepper if desired.

Makes 10 servings.

NOTE: Delicious served with a wedge of your favorite corn bread.

Rolled Apple Cobbler

This is not a traditional cobbler by any means. But it sure is delicious.

- ½ cup butter
- 1 ½ cups sugar
- 2 cups water
- 1 ½ cups self-rising flour, plus extra for rolling out pastry
- ½ cup vegetable shortening
- ⅓ cup milk
- 2 cups peeled and finely chopped apples
- 1 teaspoon cinnamon

Preheat the oven to 350 degrees. Place the butter in a 13 x 9-inch baking dish and put it in the oven to melt. When the butter is melted, remove from the oven and set aside. In a small saucepan cook the sugar and water over low heat for 3 to 5 minutes, stirring occasionally. Remove from the heat and set the sugar syrup aside.

In a medium bowl combine the flour and shortening, using your fingers to mix until a crumbly mixture forms. Add the milk and stir to make the dough. Place the dough onto a floured board. Knead until smooth. Roll the dough into an 8 x 4 x ¼-inch-thick rectangle.

In a small bowl mix the chopped apples and cinnamon together. Spread over the dough. Roll the dough jelly-roll-style from the long side. Pinch the edges together. Cut into 1-inch slices. Place cut side down in the prepared baking dish. Pour the sugar syrup over the slices. Bake for 50 minutes. Serve warm.

Makes 8 servings.

Pumpkin Cream Cheese Pie

If your family reunion occurs in December as mine does every year, then this recipe will be the perfect touch.

Cream cheese layer:
- 1 (8-ounce) package cream cheese, softened
- ⅓ cup sugar
- ½ teaspoon vanilla extract
- 1 large egg
- 1 (9-inch) deep-dish piecrust, unbaked

Pumpkin layer:
- 1 (15-ounce) can pumpkin
- ½ cup sugar
- 1 teaspoon cinnamon
- ¼ teaspoon ginger
- ⅛ teaspoon salt
- 2 large eggs, slightly beaten
- 1 cup evaporated milk

To make the cream cheese layer: Preheat the oven to 350 degrees. In a medium bowl combine the cream cheese, sugar, vanilla, and egg. Mix well and pour into the unbaked piecrust. Set aside.

To make the pumpkin layer: In a medium bowl add the pumpkin, sugar, cinnamon, ginger, and salt and stir until well combined. Blend in the beaten eggs and evaporated milk. Pour over the cream cheese layer and bake for 50 to 55 minutes or until firm.

Makes 6 to 8 servings.

Shortcake

Nothing says summer in the South like shortcake.

- ¼ cup butter
- ½ cup sugar
- 1 cup self-rising flour
- ½ cup milk
- 1 large egg, slightly beaten
- Sweetened fruit and whipped cream

Preheat the oven to 350 degrees. Place the butter in an 8-inch iron skillet and put the pan in the oven to melt the butter. In a medium bowl mix the sugar, flour, milk, and egg. Stir to combine well. Pour the melted butter over the batter and mix well. Pour the batter into the skillet. Bake for 20 to 25 minutes. Turn the cake out onto a plate.

To serve: Cut into 4 to 6 wedges, split in half. Serve with your favorite sweetened fruit and whipped cream.

Makes 4 to 6 servings.

Kelly's Banana Pudding

This is my daughter's recipe she brings to every family get-together.

- 3 (3-ounce) boxes French vanilla instant pudding mix
- 4 cups milk
- 1 cup sour cream
- 1 (14-ounce) can sweetened condensed milk
- 1 (8-ounce) container frozen whipped topping, thawed
- 10 to 12 large bananas, sliced into ¼-inch thick slices
- 2 (12-ounce) boxes vanilla wafers
- 1 (12-ounce) container frozen whipped topping, thawed

Place the pudding mix in a large bowl. Add the milk, whipping with a whisk for 3 minutes to mix well. Add the sour cream and condensed milk and mix well. Fold in the 8-ounce container of whipped topping. In a large serving dish layer the bananas, wafers, and pudding, making 2 or 3 layers. Spread the 12-ounce container of whipped topping over the top.

Makes 24 servings.

♥ CHAPTER 5 ♥

HOLIGRAZE

FROM OUR HOME
TO YOURS

On any given holiday down South, you'll find people gathered together for a meal. It might be neighbors at wooden picnic tables on the Fourth of July just before dusk, with plastic forks and patriotic-themed paper napkins. Someone will bring watermelon, and chances are there will be at least two variations of potato salad. There will be fireworks and friendship and freedom.

Or it's Easter and the extended family is coming over for lunch after church, when grandmother's deviled-egg plate is rescued from the china cabinet and the wrinkles are steamed out of the linen tablecloth. Someone will bring ham—sugar and country, because Uncle Bud will be there—and certainly yeast rolls. There will be lilies and laughter and love.

Casual or high falutin', inside or out of doors, Southerners know that food matters during the holidays. We also know that the memories matter more. Call it our secret ingredient.

♥

One Thanksgiving when my parents were out of the country, my oldest sister, Venona, who was recently married, said she'd make sure my middle sister, Lizzie, and I had a traditional meal. Lizzie, who was eighteen or so at the time, volunteered to make the dressing. Why Venona thought this might be a good idea remains a mystery some twenty years after the fact, but Lord knows that's not the only thing we don't understand about her.

Granted, Lizzie looked like she knew what she was doing as she toiled in our parents' kitchen, chopping this and measuring that. For a little extra flourish—Lizzie always was the dramatic one—she donned an apron, the kind that ties at the neck and the waist. It had pictures of Elvis Presley all over it. Lizzie tossed around words like *simmer* and *sauté*, all the while mumbling about how hard it was to read Mother's handwritten notes on the recipe card. If memory serves, she made a very big deal indeed about how mature it was of her to help Venona.

The dressing smelled fine while it was baking—edible, even—but when we took it out to get ready to drive the half hour to Venona's house, we immediately realized it didn't look like the dressing Mother always made for Thanksgiving and Christmas. And the difference was this: Lizzie's dressing was a disturbing shade of green.

In all honesty, I can't think of a shade of green dressing that wouldn't be disturbing, but this particular hue seemed especially alarming. No words were exchanged as Lizzie slapped a few pats of butter on top, covered the dish with aluminum foil, and grabbed two of the multicolored potholders I had woven at Camp DeSoto the summer before. Maybe she was hoping a little extra butter might soften the tone or fade the color a bit, but, alas, it did not.

"I'm sure it will be delicious," said Venona when we arrived at her house and she got a look at what we'd brought. She always was the diplomatic one.

It was not delicious, even if you invoked the lowest possible standard for the word. The best any of us could do was to choke down one bite apiece. Even Sloopy the dog turned up his wet nose, and he had a neighborhood-wide reputation for eating out of garbage cans.

Thankfully—and, after all, it was Thanksgiving—other guests had provided a veritable smorgasbord of casseroles: sweet potato, squash, green bean, and something Mrs. Willis from across the street described as "kitchen sink surprise." Don't ask me what was in it, because we were sworn to silence. I will say, however, that it was delicious. So there was plenty to take the place of the dressing—did I mention the cheese grits?—and no one seemed to mind. At least no one said so out loud, it being Alabama and us being so polite and all.

Since then Lizzie has been encouraged to provide sweet tea for our family holiday meals. Sometimes at Christmas, if we're feeling lucky, we let her bring seven-layer salad, because Venona—bless her heart—steadfastly believes just about anyone can be trusted to put peas on top of lettuce.

At the end of the day, the green dressing didn't really matter. We walked away with more than full stomachs. We created a memory that still makes us laugh after two decades of retelling and keeps our hearts full of gratitude for one another.

Almond Iced Tea

Be careful when using the almond extract. One teaspoon might not seem like a lot, but it is very potent.

         4   regular size tea bags
         1   cup boiling water
    1 ½   cups sugar
         4   cups water
       ¾   cup lemon juice
         1   teaspoon almond extract
         1   (32-ounce) bottle ginger ale

Place the tea bags in a heatproof container and cover with the boiling water. Let the tea steep for 5 minutes. Remove the tea bags. Add the sugar, water, lemon juice, and almond extract. Place in the refrigerator to chill. Add the ginger ale when you're ready to serve. Serve over ice.

Makes ½ gallon.

Elizabeth's No-Boil Boiled Custard

This is my oldest sister's recipe. It is a Christmas tradition in our family.

         3   quarts milk
         2   (3-ounce) boxes vanilla instant pudding
       ¾   cup sugar
         1   teaspoon vanilla extract
         1   (8-ounce) container frozen whipped topping, thawed

Place the milk and instant pudding in a large bowl. Whisk together for 5 minutes. Add the sugar and vanilla and stir. Fold in the thawed whipped topping. Place in the refrigerator until serving time.

Makes 30 (4-ounce) servings.

Potato Salad the Way Your Mother Made It

If you are serving this at a summer holiday gathering, be sure to keep it chilled if it is going to be sitting out longer than two hours.

9	medium baking potatoes, scrubbed
4	large boiled eggs, chopped
½	cup chopped sweet pickles
½	cup chopped dill pickles
¼	cup minced onions
½	cup diced red bell pepper
1	teaspoon salt
½	teaspoon black pepper
1	to 1 ½ cups mayonnaise
1	tablespoon mustard
¼	cup stuffed olives, sliced

Place the unpeeled potatoes in a large stockpot and cover with water by 1 inch. Bring to a boil, reduce the heat, and simmer for 25 minutes or until tender. Drain and let cool enough to peel and chop into 1-inch cubes. In a large bowl place the chopped potatoes, eggs, sweet pickles, dill pickles, onion, red bell pepper, salt, and pepper, and stir gently to mix. Add the mayonnaise and mustard, stirring carefully so you do not mash the potatoes. Garnish with the sliced olives. Cover and place in the refrigerator until serving time.

Makes 10 to 12 servings.

Ambrosia

You can't have Christmas without ambrosia.

12	large navel oranges
½	cup sugar
2	cups freshly grated coconut

Peel and section the oranges, slicing in between each membrane. In a serving bowl layer ½ the oranges, ½ the sugar, and ½ the coconut and then repeat using the remaining ingredients. Cover and cool in the refrigerator for 2 hours before serving.

Makes 6 servings.

Melt in Your Mouth Corn Bread

I am a Southern cook and I have a corn bread recipe for almost every occasion. Yes, this one has a lot of butter in it. But it does just melt in your mouth. And for real Southerners, this is great crumbled in milk.

- ½ cup self-rising flour
- ½ cup self-rising cornmeal
- ½ cup buttermilk
- 2 large eggs, slightly beaten
- ½ cup butter

Preheat the oven to 400 degrees. In a medium bowl combine the flour and cornmeal. Add the buttermilk and eggs, stirring to mix well. Melt the butter in a 9-inch skillet over medium heat. When melted, pour the butter over the corn bread mixture and stir well. Return the corn bread batter to the skillet and bake for 20 minutes or until golden brown.

To serve: You can remove the corn bread from the skillet when you take it out of the oven or serve from the skillet if you prefer.

Makes 12 servings.

Succotash

Growing up we always had corn and lima beans in our garden. The combination of these two vegetables is wonderful.

2 cups lima beans, fresh or frozen
2 cups whole kernel corn, fresh or frozen
1 cup milk
¼ cup butter
½ teaspoon salt
½ teaspoon black pepper

In a medium saucepan combine the lima beans, corn, and milk. Simmer over medium heat for about 20 minutes or until the vegetables are tender, stirring occasionally. Add the butter, salt, and pepper. Stir well and pour into a serving dish.

Makes 6 servings.

Buttermilk Pie with Pecans

In the rural South families always had butter, buttermilk, and eggs on hand. This recipe has been around for more than a hundred years and for good reason.

½ cup butter
1 ½ cups sugar
3 large eggs, beaten
½ cup buttermilk
2 tablespoons all-purpose flour
2 teaspoons vanilla extract
1 cup pecan halves
1 (9-inch) unbaked piecrust

Preheat the oven to 350 degrees.

Place the butter and sugar in a medium bowl. Using an electric mixer cream until well mixed. Add in the beaten eggs, mixing well. Stir in the buttermilk, flour, vanilla, and pecan halves. Pour into the piecrust. Bake for 50 minutes or until firm to the touch. Cool for 30 minutes before serving.

Makes 1 pie or 6 to 8 servings.

Traditional Southern Corn Bread Dressing

While a tradition at Thanksgiving and Christmas, this is good all year long. It's really good with chicken as well as turkey.

Corn bread:
- 2 cups self-rising cornmeal
- ¼ cup self-rising flour
- 2 cups buttermilk
- 2 large eggs
- ¾ cup finely chopped celery
- ½ cup finely chopped onion
- 2 tablespoons bacon drippings

Dressing:
- 8 cups crumbled corn bread
- 4 cups cubed stale white bread
- 4 cups hot chicken or turkey broth (or pan drippings from baked chicken or turkey)
- 1 (10.75-ounce) can cream of chicken soup
- ¾ tablespoon rubbed sage
- ½ teaspoon black pepper

To make the corn bread: Preheat the oven to 400 degrees. Grease a 9-inch cast-iron skillet and set aside. In a large bowl combine the cornmeal and flour. Add the buttermilk, eggs, celery, onion, and bacon drippings. Stir to mix well. Pour into the prepared skillet and bake for 20 minutes or until firm to the touch and golden brown. Let sit for 10 to 15 minutes and then crumble for the dressing.

To make the dressing: Preheat the oven to 400 degrees. Grease a 13 x 9-inch casserole dish and set aside. In a large bowl add the corn bread, white bread cubes, broth, cream of chicken soup, sage, and pepper. Stir to mix well and pour into the prepared casserole dish. Bake for 40 to 45 minutes.

Makes 10 to 12 servings.

NOTE: This corn bread recipe was created just to use in this dressing. When crumbled it will give you the 8 cups you need to make the dressing.

Sweet P (Potato and Pineapple) Casserole

The combination of the sweet potatoes and pineapple gives this an extra punch you don't find in most sweet potato casseroles.

- 3 medium sweet potatoes
- 2 large eggs, well beaten
- ⅔ cup evaporated milk
- 1 cup sugar
- 1 (20-ounce) can crushed pineapple, drained
- 1 cup pecans, divided
- 2 cups miniature marshmallows
- 1 cup firmly packed brown sugar
- 6 tablespoons butter
- 2 cups corn flakes

Preheat the oven to 350 degrees. Grease a 13 x 9-inch baking dish and set aside. Peel the sweet potatoes, cut into 2-inch cubes, and place in a medium saucepan. Cover the sweet potatoes with water and bring to a boil over high heat. Reduce heat and simmer for 20 minutes, or until tender. Drain the sweet potatoes, place them in a large bowl, and mash. Add the eggs, evaporated milk, sugar, pineapple, ½ cup of the pecans, and the marshmallows. Pour into the prepared baking dish. Bake for 20 minutes.

In a small bowl mix together the brown sugar, butter, corn flakes, and the remaining ½ cup pecans until it reaches a crumbly mixture. Place on top of the sweet potatoes and bake for an additional 15 to 20 minutes.

Makes 10 servings.

Country Green Beans with Baby Red Potatoes

This is just as country as corn bread.

- ¼ pound bacon or hog jowl
- 1 quart water, plus more as needed
- 2 quarts green beans, snapped with the tips and ends removed, cut into 1 ½-inch pieces
- 1 small onion, quartered (optional)
- 2 teaspoons salt
- 12 small red potatoes, scrubbed (peeling left on)

Add the bacon and water to a 4-quart Dutch oven. Cover and simmer for 30 minutes. Add the green beans, onion, and salt. Simmer the beans for 2 hours, adding more water as necessary. Add the potatoes, cover, and continue to simmer over medium heat for 1 hour. Remove the cover and continue cooking until the liquid has reduced.

Makes 8 servings.

Patsy's Chicken Salad

This chicken salad has a number of ingredients you don't usually find in chicken salad. I think the addition of the lettuce, onion, and cheddar cheese makes this so much better than what you get in stores.

- 4 cups diced, cooked chicken
- 1 tablespoon lemon juice
- 1 cup pecans, chopped
- 1 cup shredded lettuce
- 1 cup shredded cheddar cheese
- 1 medium-size tomato, diced
- 2 tablespoons finely diced green onion
- 1 to 1 ½ cups mayonnaise

Place the chicken in a large bowl. Add the lemon juice and stir to coat the chicken. Add the chopped pecans, lettuce, cheese, tomato, green onion, and mayonnaise. Stir to mix well. Cover and place in the refrigerator.

To serve: Serve as a sandwich filling, in a tortilla wrap, as an accompaniment to a salad, or stuffed in a tomato.

Makes 6 cups.

NOTE: Feel free to pick up a rotisserie chicken if you're short on time.

Roasted Turkey

No one should be afraid of roasting a turkey.

1 (10- to 12-pound) turkey
½ cup butter, softened
2 tablespoons chopped parsley
1 tablespoon finely chopped fresh thyme
2 teaspoons finely chopped rubbed sage
2 teaspoons black pepper
2 teaspoons salt
1 small onion, quartered
1 large carrot, quartered
1 large stalk celery, quartered
4 cups chicken broth

Preheat the oven to 450 degrees. Place a wire rack in a large roasting pan and spray with nonstick cooking spray. Rinse the turkey with cold water and pat dry with paper towels. Save the giblet packet and the turkey neck for giblet gravy (page 108).

In a small bowl mix the butter, parsley, thyme, sage, pepper, and salt to make a paste. Rub the paste inside the cavity of the turkey as well as on the skin. Tie the legs together and tuck the wing tips underneath. Place breast side up on the rack. Add the onion, carrot, celery, and chicken broth to the pan. Roast for 20 minutes. Reduce the heat to 325 degrees and baste every 20 minutes until the thermometer reaches 175 degrees, about 3 hours. Let the turkey rest 30 minutes before carving. Reserve the pan drippings for the corn bread dressing (page 101).

Makes 10 to 12 servings.

Giblet Gravy

This traditional gravy is the reason the good Lord gave us gravy boats. You will use your gravy boat at least once a year at Thanksgiving.

Giblet bag and turkey neck from Roasted Turkey recipe (page 107)
2 cups chicken broth (canned or homemade)
1 ⅓ cups water, divided
¼ cup chopped onion
¼ cup chopped celery
½ teaspoon salt, plus additional if needed
¼ teaspoon black pepper, plus additional if needed
1 ½ tablespoons all-purpose flour
2 large hard-boiled eggs, chopped

Place the gizzard, liver, and turkey neck in a medium saucepan. Add the chicken broth and 1 cup of the water. Bring to a boil over high heat and then reduce the heat to low and simmer for 1 hour. Add the onion, celery, salt, and pepper, and continue to simmer for 45 minutes. Remove from the heat and strain the liquid into a bowl, reserving the gizzard and liver. Pour the remaining liquid back into the saucepan, about 2 to 2 ½ cups. Chop the gizzard and liver and add to the broth. Dissolve the flour in the remaining ⅓ cup water. Add to the broth and bring to a boil, boiling for 2 to 3 minutes. Add the hard-boiled eggs. Taste for seasoning, adding more salt and pepper if needed.

Makes 3 cups.

Sister's Granny Smith Apple Pie with Cream Cheese Piecrust

I am the youngest of nine children and one of five girls in my family. My sister Juanita was a great cook and she shared this recipe with me more than thirty years ago.

Piecrust:
- 1 cup butter, softened
- 1 (8-ounce) package cream cheese, softened
- 2 ¼ cups all-purpose flour
- ½ teaspoon salt

Filling:
- ½ cup butter
- 1 cup sugar
- 1 tablespoon flour
- ¼ cup orange juice
- ¼ cup honey
- ½ teaspoon cinnamon
- 4 cups peeled and thinly sliced Granny Smith apples

To make the piecrust: In a large bowl cream the butter and cream cheese. Gradually blend in the flour and salt. Knead lightly until the dough clings together. Divide in half. Wrap each half in plastic wrap and refrigerate for 30 minutes. Place one ball of dough on a lightly floured board and roll into a 10-inch circle to fit a 9-inch pie pan. Roll the remaining crust into a 10-inch circle. Cut into ½-inch-wide strips and set aside.

To make the filling and assemble the pie: Preheat the oven to 450 degrees. In a large saucepan melt the butter over low heat. Add the sugar, flour, orange juice, honey, and cinnamon, stirring to mix. Add the apples and cook over medium heat for 10 minutes. Pour into the prepared piecrust.

Crisscross the strips from the second piecrust across the top of the apple mixture in a latticework pattern. Place in the oven and bake for 10 minutes. Reduce the heat to 350 degrees and continue to bake for 45 minutes.

Makes 1 pie or 6 to 8 servings.

Easy Easter Leg of Lamb

For an even easier version of this recipe try using a boneless leg of lamb.

2 teaspoons minced garlic
1 tablespoon paprika
1 tablespoon salt
1 teaspoon dried rosemary
1 teaspoon dried thyme
1 teaspoon dried oregano
1 teaspoon black pepper
1 (5- to 6-pound) leg of lamb, trimmed of fat
⅓ cup olive oil

Preheat the oven to 400 degrees. Place a rack in a 10 x 16 x 2-inch roasting pan. In a small bowl combine the garlic, paprika, salt, rosemary, thyme, oregano, and pepper. Make slits on the lamb and rub the mixture into the slits and over the outside of the surface. Rub with the olive oil. Place on the rack. Roast uncovered for 1 ½ to 2 hours or until a meat thermometer registers 140 degrees for medium.

To serve: Carve the lamb into thin slices.

Makes 10 to 12 servings.

NOTE: Most grocery stores stock boneless legs of lamb around Easter.

Boiled Tennessee Country Ham

Every good Southern cook needs to know how to prepare this. Country ham is a tradition for the holidays in our home and there are so many different uses for it.

1 country ham (15 to 18 pounds)

Have the butcher cut the hock end from the ham, leaving about 10 inches of the ham to boil. Place in a large pot and cover with water to soak for 24 hours. Change the water every 12 hours. When you're ready to cook, place the soaked ham in another large pot and cover with water. Bring to a boil, reduce the heat, and simmer for 20 minutes per pound. Turn off the heat and let the ham cool in the liquid. Transfer to a platter and remove the skin and fat. Place in the refrigerator until cold, then cut into thin slices.

Makes 30 servings.

Thanksgiving Pie

This is another great way to work cranberries into your holiday menus.

2 tablespoons all-purpose flour, divided
2 (9-inch) unbaked piecrusts
1 cup cranberries
¾ cup chopped walnuts
1 medium apple, chopped (1 cup)
¾ cup raisins
1 cup firmly packed brown sugar
½ cup cranberry juice
¼ cup butter

Preheat the oven to 400 degrees. Sprinkle 1 tablespoon of the flour over one piecrust and set aside. In a medium bowl toss the cranberries, walnuts, chopped apples, and raisins. Add the brown sugar, the remaining 1 tablespoon flour, and the cranberry juice and mix well. Pour the filling into the prepared crust and dot with the butter. Cut the remaining crust into ½-inch strips. Place the strips across the pie in a latticework pattern. Bake for 30 to 45 minutes or until the crust is brown and the juices are bubbling.

Makes 8 servings.

Baked Perfect Peach Pie

This is a great way to use fresh peaches.

1 cup sugar
5 tablespoons all-purpose flour
⅛ teaspoon salt
1 (9-inch) piecrust, unbaked
4 fresh peaches, peeled and cut in half
1 cup heavy cream

Preheat the oven to 400 degrees. In a small bowl mix the sugar, flour, and salt. Sprinkle ½ of the mixture over the unbaked piecrust. Place the peaches, cut side up, on top of the flour mixture in the piecrust. Mix the heavy cream with the remaining sugar and flour mixture and pour over the peaches. Bake for 15 minutes, reduce the heat to 350 degrees and continue to bake for an additional 1 hour and 15 minutes.

Makes 1 pie or 6 to 8 servings.

♥ CHAPTER 6 ♥
TAILGATING

WE'VE GOT CUPCAKES,
YES WE DO

Clara knows full well that some people think college football is all about the game. Her husband, Harrison Sanders—Harris for short—is one of them. All Harris can talk about during the season is starting lineups, well-executed touchdown passes, and how soon one player or another will get off the injured list. Poor thing, the way Harris goes on and on about Bear Bryant, you'd think the legendary coach was still alive and calling plays on the field. But Clara knows that for some people, herself included, college football is about the game *and* the getting together.

Her mama taught her early on about the art of the tailgate, and that training served her well in college. Today, now that she and Harris have graduated and are raising children of their own, Clara is more determined than ever to continue the tradition. There's not a home game that goes by that you won't find the Sanders brood on campus, and they try to make it to at least one away game every fall.

Southerners make it look easy, but in reality both well-honed culinary skills and top-notch social savvy are required for successful tailgating. You need to know how to cook, yes. You need to know which foods will travel without going bad. And you have to accept that being on the road is no excuse for poor presentation.

But you must also be able to handle that roommate you never really got along with when she parades by before the game to show off her handsome husband and three perfect children and pictures of their most recent trip to Italy.

"Well bless your heart," she'll say when Clara responds with her own vacation story about two weeks in a fully furnished cabin in Gatlinburg over the summer. "That's so dear," the mean woman will add. "And local." Please, whatever you do, don't get Clara started on her.

And you might as well be ready to run into the sociology professor who treated you so unfairly when you were late for class two weeks in a row because of rush. As vice-president of the sorority, you had obligations. You tried to explain it to him, but he did not seem to appreciate the seriousness with which you undertook your commitment to the next generation of sisters.

♥

Back in Clara's grandmother's day, an old quilt and a mess of fried chicken might have done the trick. And Clara can accept that some fans still prefer the cardboard-table-out-of-the trunk approach. She understands that's how the concept originated, eating a picnic on the tailgate of the car. If you push her, Clara will even acknowl-edge the growing number of tailgaters who park their RVs near the campus the night before the game, setting up their grills and tuning in their radios early the next morning. That's a tad too rustic for Clara's taste, sort of like camping out. It's quaint, though, and who is Clara to mock someone's tailgating preferences?

As for Clara and her ilk, they prefer to be on campus, in the middle of the action. The Sanderses like to set up their tent in front of the old law school, because it's a prime spot for seeing the players run by on their way to the stadium. It makes Harris happy, being so close to the athletes for those few, brief moments. He hadn't been eli-gible to play himself, and if you must know, Clara isn't convinced he's dealt with that particular dis-appointment in a healthy manner. So she asked her daddy to do what he could to reserve that spot on the quad for them in perpetuity. She doesn't make a habit of it, of course, but sometimes Clara is forced to take advantage of her connections. Her father worked hard to get into the school's contributors hall of fame, after all, so why not capitalize on it once in a while? That's Clara's phi-losophy at least. You might feel different.

On the morning of every home game, Clara shakes out the tablecloth, the one her mother-in-law had specially designed in school colors, and lets it settle over the long folding table she found on the "last chance aisle" at Lucky's Bargain Bin. (Even though the Sanderses are blessed financially, Clara still appreciates a good deal as much as anyone.) Depending on what she's serving that day, she'll either light the Sterno to keep the beef tenderloin warm or spread the ice evenly over the shrimp. Her mama never did resort to plastic utensils, so it's standard issue for Clara to use real silverware. It complements the chilled pewter cups she brings for the mint tea. Some of her friends use disposable everything: cups, plates, napkins, knives, and forks; and a few are raving about some newfangled biodegradable bamboo plates you can throw right on your compost pile. All that's fine, of course. But Clara sees no reason to change her tailgating philosophy at this stage of the game.

"We called them 'picnics,'" says Clara's grandmother every time she sees Clara getting ready for an upcoming game. "We didn't need monogrammed napkins and imported cheese like you young people do today. We had team spirit and hot dogs. Maybe a little blackberry lemonade, if we were lucky. But sugar was so expensive back then . . ."

Such naysaying does not faze Clara in the least. She's too busy making tiny goalposts out of icing for the cupcakes and tossing the black bean and corn salsa. It's no bother, really, because Clara is proud of her heritage and she wants to pass that respect on to her children. They may not appreciate it now, being so young and all, but one day they'll be thankful they had a mother who cared enough to teach them how to carve a football out of a pumpkin for the tailgate center-piece. Clara is sure of it.

Orange Blush

This punch is perfect for those late summer tailgate parties.

 1 (12-ounce) can frozen orange juice concentrate, thawed
 2 cups cranberry juice
 ½ cup sugar
 1 quart ginger ale

In a large pitcher combine the undiluted orange juice, cranberry juice, and sugar. Add the ginger ale, stir well, and chill. Serve over ice.

Makes 8 servings.

Hunk-a Hunk-a Barbecued Bologna

In the South, bologna is sometimes referred to as "poor man's steak." But this is one of the richest, most flavorful cuts of meat I serve at parties.

 3 to 4 pounds unsliced bologna
 ½ cup butter
    Juice of 2 lemons
 1 cup chili sauce
 2 teaspoons Worcestershire sauce
    Party rye bread (optional)
    Swiss cheese (optional)
    Mustard (optional)

Preheat the oven to 250 degrees. Score the bologna on all sides and place in a 13 x 9-inch baking dish. In a small dish combine the butter, lemon juice, chili sauce, and Worcestershire sauce, stirring to mix well. Cover the bologna with the sauce. Place in the oven and bake for 3 hours, basting often to prevent drying.

To serve: Remove bologna to a serving platter. Cover with the sauce from the baking dish. Allow your guests to cut their own slices of the bologna. Serve with party rye bread, Swiss cheese, and a dish of mustard if desired.

Makes 10 to 12 servings.

Rosemary Roasted Cashews

With every tailgate group, there is always at least one straggler. This is something the people who showed up on time can enjoy while waiting for the rest of the food to arrive. But don't take too much of this, because people will ruin their dinner—it is that addictive.

- 3 tablespoons butter, plus extra for the baking sheet
- 2 pounds whole roasted cashews
- 2 tablespoons firmly packed light brown sugar
- 3 tablespoons chopped fresh rosemary
- ½ teaspoon cayenne pepper

Preheat the oven to 375 degrees. Grease a 15 x 10-inch baking pan with butter and spread the cashews on it. Bake for 5 minutes. In a large Dutch oven melt the remaining 3 tablespoons butter over medium heat. Add the brown sugar, stirring to dissolve. Remove from the heat and add the rosemary and cayenne pepper. Add the cashews to the Dutch oven and toss to coat evenly. Spread the cashews on the baking pan again and bake for an additional 8 to 10 minutes, or until lightly browned, stirring occasionally.

Makes 6 cups.

NOTE: Store in an airtight container.

Hotter than a Pepper Sprout Corn Muffins

This is so good with barbecue, you may never buy another bun in your life.

- 1 ½ cups self-rising cornmeal
- 1 cup shredded cheddar cheese
- 1 (14.75-ounce) can creamed corn
- ⅔ cup vegetable oil
- 1 cup buttermilk
- 3 large eggs
- ½ cup finely diced green bell pepper
- 2 jalapeño peppers, seeded and finely diced

Preheat the oven to 350 degrees. Grease two 12-cup muffin pans and set aside. In a large bowl combine the cornmeal, cheddar cheese, corn, vegetable oil, buttermilk, eggs, bell pepper, and jalapeño peppers. Stir to mix well. Spoon the batter into the prepared muffin cups, filling each cup ⅔ full. Bake for 30 minutes or until golden brown.

Makes 24 muffins.

Tennessee Caviar

This is wonderful with corn chips or on a toasted baguette.

     2 (15-ounce) cans black-eyed peas, rinsed and drained
     1 (15-ounce) can yellow hominy, drained
     ½ cup chopped green bell pepper
     ½ cup chopped red bell pepper
     1 cup finely chopped onion
     1 cup chopped tomato
     ½ cup chopped green onions
     ¼ cup chopped jalapeño pepper
     ¼ cup chopped cilantro
     1 (16-ounce) jar picante sauce
     2 teaspoons sugar
     1 tablespoon cumin
     1 teaspoon salt
     2 teaspoons black pepper

In a large bowl combine the black-eyed peas, hominy, the green and the red bell peppers, onion, tomato, green onions, jalapeño pepper, and cilantro. Stir to mix well. Add the picante sauce, sugar, cumin, salt, and pepper. Mix well. Cover and chill 8 hours or longer.

Makes 20 servings.

Pepper Jack Spinach Dip

If you are like me you have tried dozens of spinach dip recipes. This one gets the biggest hurrahs from my guests.

1 (10-ounce) package frozen spinach, thawed and drained
1 (8-ounce) package cream cheese, softened
½ cup finely diced onion
1 large tomato, finely diced
⅓ cup half-and-half
2 cups shredded Pepper Jack cheese
   Raw vegetables or chips for serving

Preheat the oven to 350 degrees. Spray a 9-inch-square baking dish with nonstick cooking spray and set aside. In a medium bowl add the spinach, cream cheese, onion, tomato, half-and-half, and Pepper Jack cheese. Stir, mixing well, and pour into the prepared baking dish. Bake for 25 minutes. Serve with raw vegetables or chips.

Makes 8 to 10 servings.

Bacon and Tomato Biscuit Tarts

These are great for those late-morning fall football games.

1 (16.3-ounce, 8 count) can flaky layer biscuits
8 slices bacon, fried and crumbled
1 (10-ounce) can diced tomatoes and green chilies
1 cup shredded Monterey Jack cheese
½ cup mayonnaise
½ teaspoon dried basil leaves
½ teaspoon dried thyme
½ teaspoon dried oregano
½ teaspoon garlic salt

Preheat the oven to 375 degrees. Lightly spray two 12-cup muffin tins with nonstick cooking spray. Pull the layers of each biscuit apart to form three pieces. Press each piece into a muffin cup. In a medium bowl combine the bacon, diced tomatoes, cheese, mayonnaise, basil, thyme, oregano, and garlic salt, stirring to mix well. Spoon 1 tablespoon of the mixture into each prepared muffin cup. Bake for 10 to 12 minutes or until golden brown.

Makes 24 servings.

Baby Red Potatoes Stuffed with Cheese

I have been serving this at parties for more than twenty years. Without fail, this is always the first thing to go.

- 18 small red potatoes, scrubbed
- ¾ cup mayonnaise
- 1 ¼ cups shredded cheddar cheese
- ¼ cup grated Parmesan cheese
- ½ teaspoon salt
- ½ teaspoon black pepper

Preheat the oven to 425 degrees. Split the potatoes in half lengthwise and trim the bottom of each half so they sit flat. Using a small scoop, hollow out the middle of each half and discard. Place the potato halves in a large saucepan. Cover with water by 2 inches. Bring to a boil and cook until just tender. Remove, drain, and cool. In a medium bowl combine the mayonnaise, cheddar cheese, Parmesan cheese, salt, and pepper. Spoon the mixture into the potatoes to fill each hole. Bake for about 10 minutes or until the cheese becomes golden brown.

Makes 12 servings.

Cabbage and Corn Slaw

This is an excellent side dish for barbecue.

- 3 cups shredded cabbage (about one small head)
- 1 (14-ounce) can whole kernel corn, drained
- ½ cup finely chopped onion
- ½ cup finely chopped green pepper
- ½ cup chopped red bell pepper
- ½ cup finely chopped celery
- ½ cup chopped sweet pickles
- ½ cup mayonnaise
- ¼ teaspoon salt
- ¼ teaspoon black pepper

In a large bowl combine the cabbage, corn, onion, green and red peppers, celery, pickles, mayonnaise, salt, and pepper. Mix well. Cover and chill for 2 hours before serving.

Makes 8 servings.

NOTE: Those of you who are adventurous might want to try some on a barbecue sandwich.

Chili Cheese Pie

This delicious dish resembles a cheesecake when finished. Just scoop with tortilla chips for some delicious tailgate fare.

1   cup crushed tortilla chips
3   tablespoons melted butter
2   (8-ounce) packages cream cheese, softened
2   large eggs
1   (4-ounce) can chopped green chilies
2   jalapeño peppers, minced
1   cup shredded cheddar cheese
1   cup shredded Monterey Jack cheese
½   cup sour cream
¼   cup chopped green onions for garnish
½   cup chopped tomatoes for garnish
½   cup chopped black olives for garnish
    Tortilla chips for serving

Preheat the oven to 325 degrees. Grease the bottom and sides of a 9-inch springform pan and set aside. In a small bowl mix the crushed tortilla chips and butter. Press the mixture over the bottom of the prepared pan. Bake for 15 minutes. In a large bowl beat the cream cheese and eggs. Stir in the green chilies, jalapeño peppers, and cheddar and Monterey Jack cheeses. Pour over the baked layer and bake for and additional 30 minutes. Remove from the oven and cool for 5 minutes. Loosen the side of the pan and place the cheese pie on a serving plate. Garnish with green onions, tomatoes, and olives. Chill 1 hour before serving.

Makes 12 servings.

Double Threat Pickled Shrimp

One reason I love this recipe is that not only is this dish delicious, but it is also so attractive when you serve it.

2	to 2 ½ pounds shrimp, cooked and peeled
1	medium onion, thinly sliced into rings
1	lemon, thinly sliced
3	bay leaves
1	(10.75-ounce) can tomato soup
½	cup apple cider vinegar
½	teaspoon paprika
1	teaspoon crushed red pepper flakes
½	teaspoon dry mustard
½	teaspoon garlic powder
1 ½	teaspoons Worcestershire sauce
1	teaspoon salt
1	large green bell pepper, sliced into rings

In a large bowl combine the shrimp, onion, lemon slices, and bay leaves. In a medium bowl combine the tomato soup, vinegar, paprika, red pepper flakes, dry mustard, garlic powder, Worcestershire sauce, and salt and pour over the shrimp mixture. Refrigerate overnight.

To serve: Remove the bay leaves and place the shrimp in a large glass serving bowl. Garnish with green pepper rings.

Makes 10 to 12 servings.

NOTE: Even if you are putting out the food at your party on an actual tailgate of an old pickup truck, you can put this in your best silver serving dish and bring some class to the party.

Hot Chicken Wings

I think there must be a law in the South about serving chicken wings at a tailgate party.

     Oil for frying
 2   pounds chicken wings
 ½   cup all-purpose flour
 1   teaspoon salt
 ½   teaspoon black pepper
 ⅓   cup butter, melted
 3   tablespoons hot sauce of your choice
     Celery sticks for dipping
     Blue cheese dressing

Pour the oil into a Dutch oven or large pot and bring to 350 degrees over high heat. Remove and discard the wing tip and separate each wing into 2 pieces. In a medium bowl combine the flour, salt, and pepper. Coat the drumettes and wings with the flour mixture. Fry each batch in a single layer for 10 minutes, being careful not to crowd the pan. Remove to a platter and keep warm while frying the remaining drumettes and wings. In a small bowl mix the butter and hot sauce together and pour over the cooked pieces. Toss to coat each piece evenly. Serve with celery sticks and blue cheese dressing.

Makes 10 to 12 servings.

Steak Sandwiches with Corn Relish

This recipe combines two of my favorite flavors.

Steak:
- 2 (each about 1 pound) flank steaks
- ¼ cup olive oil
- 1 tablespoon cumin
- 1 tablespoon chili powder
- 2 teaspoons salt
- 2 teaspoons black pepper
- 1 teaspoon coriander
- ¼ teaspoon cayenne pepper
- 1 teaspoon paprika
- ½ teaspoon crushed red pepper flakes

Corn relish:
- 2 cups whole kernel corn, fresh or frozen
- 1 ½ teaspoons salt
- ½ teaspoon black pepper
- 1 cup finely chopped red onion
- 1 cup finely chopped red bell pepper
- 1 (4-ounce) can mild green chilies, drained and chopped
- ½ cup apple cider vinegar
- ⅓ cup firmly packed brown sugar
- 1 teaspoon mustard seeds
- 2 teaspoons finely chopped garlic
- 18 small sourdough rolls

To make the steak: Rub the flank steaks with olive oil. In a small bowl combine the cumin, chili powder, salt, black pepper, coriander, cayenne pepper, paprika, and crushed red pepper flakes. Sprinkle over the flank steaks. Cover and chill 1 hour before cooking.

Put the steaks on a roasting pan and broil 7 inches from the heat source for 7 minutes. Turn the steaks over and broil for an additional 6 minutes. Remove from the oven. Cover with foil and let rest for 15 minutes. When ready to prepare sandwiches, thinly slice steaks across the grain.

To make the corn relish: In a large saucepan over high heat, add the corn, salt, and pepper. Brown the corn slightly for about 2 minutes, stirring constantly. Add the onion, red bell pepper, green chilies, vinegar, brown sugar, mustard seeds, and garlic. Let the mixture come to a boil. Lower the heat and simmer for 30 to 40 minutes or until almost all the liquid has evaporated. Refrigerate.

To assemble the sandwiches: Cut the rolls in half and scoop out the center, leaving the hollowed-out shells. Place slices of beef over the bottom half and spread the corn relish over the meat. Cover with the top half of the roll and serve.

Makes 18 servings.

NOTE: The corn relish can be made 2 or 3 days ahead and kept refrigerated.

Barbecued Boston Butt Roast with Barbecue Sauce

If there is ever another Civil War in the United States, there is a good chance it will be over barbecue and barbecue sauce. This is a Carolina-influenced sauce, and it is my personal favorite.

Barbecue:

- 6 cups wood chips, preferably hickory
- 1 ½ tablespoons paprika
- 1 tablespoon firmly packed brown sugar
- 1 tablespoon salt
- 2 teaspoons black pepper
- 1 teaspoon dry mustard
- 1 teaspoon garlic powder
- ½ teaspoon cayenne pepper
- 1 (7- to 9-pound) Boston butt roast (bone-in)

Sauce:

- 2 cups apple cider vinegar
- ½ cup ketchup
- ¼ cup firmly packed brown sugar
- 1 tablespoon salt
- 1 tablespoon black pepper
- 2 teaspoons crushed red pepper flakes

To make the barbecue: Prepare the smoker or grill according to directions. If using a smoker box soak the wood chips for 30 minutes before adding to the box. In a small bowl place the paprika, brown sugar, salt, pepper, mustard, garlic powder, and cayenne pepper and stir to mix. Sprinkle the rub over the meat, covering well. Cut slits in the meat and sprinkle the rub deep inside.

Cook on prepared smoker or grill at medium-low heat for approximately 6 hours, adding more wood to the smoker box as necessary. The internal temperature should be 195 degrees. Let the pork rest for 30 minutes and then pull apart. Cover. Serve with barbecue sauce.

To make the sauce: In a small bowl combine the vinegar, ketchup, brown sugar, salt, black pepper, and red pepper flakes. Whisk until the sugar and salt are dissolved. Pour in a jar and place in the refrigerator. The sauce will keep for several weeks.

Makes 12 to 14 servings. (Makes 2 ½ cups sauce.)

NOTE: Feel free to substitute your own favorite barbeque sauce. My feelings won't be hurt in the least.

Red Velvet Cupcakes

Everyone will love these delicious cupcakes. But especially Alabama, Arkansas, Georgia, Mississippi State, and Ole Miss fans. Play with the food coloring to get as close to your school colors as you can.

Cupcakes:
- 2 ¼ cups cake flour
- 1 tablespoon baking cocoa
- 1 teaspoon salt
- 1 teaspoon baking soda
- 1 cup buttermilk
- 2 teaspoons white vinegar
- ½ cup vegetable shortening
- 1 ½ cups sugar
- 2 large eggs
- 1 (1-ounce) bottle red food coloring
- 1 teaspoon vanilla extract

Icing:
- 1 (8-ounce) package cream cheese, softened
- ½ cup butter, softened
- 3 ½ cups powdered sugar
- 1 ½ teaspoons vanilla extract

To prepare the cupcakes: Preheat the oven to 350 degrees. Prepare two 12-cup muffin pans with paper liners or spray with nonstick cooking spray and set aside. In a large bowl mix the flour, baking cocoa, and salt. In a small bowl dissolve the baking soda in the buttermilk and vinegar. Set both bowls aside.

In the bowl of your mixer beat the shortening on medium speed until light and fluffy. Gradually add the sugar, continuing to beat. Add the eggs one at a time. Add the food coloring and vanilla. Reduce the speed to low and add the dry ingredients alternately with the buttermilk mixture, beginning and ending with the dry ingredients. Fill the prepared muffin tins ⅔ full. Bake for 20 to 25 minutes or until a wooden toothpick comes out clean. Cool completely before icing.

To prepare the icing: Place the cream cheese and butter in a large bowl. Using a hand mixer beat the mixture until light and fluffy. Gradually add the sugar and vanilla and continue to beat on low speed until smooth.

To serve: Spread the icing on top of the cooled cupcakes.

Makes 24 cupcakes.

Big Orange Cheesecake

Great for fans of Auburn, Florida, and the UTs (Tennessee and Texas).

Crust:
- 1 ½ cups graham cracker crumbs
- 1 teaspoon grated orange rind
- 3 tablespoons melted butter

Filling:
- 4 (8-ounce) packages cream cheese, softened
- 1 cup finely shredded cheddar cheese
- ¼ cup all-purpose flour
- 1 ½ cups sugar
- 5 large eggs
- ¼ cup orange juice
- ½ cup heavy cream
- ½ teaspoon grated orange rind
- 1 teaspoon vanilla extract

Orange sauce:
- 1 cup sugar
- ⅓ cup all-purpose flour
- ⅛ teaspoon salt
- 2 teaspoons grated orange rind
- ½ cup fresh orange juice
- 2 tablespoons lemon juice
- 3 large egg yolks
- 2 teaspoons butter
- 1 cup heavy whipping cream

To make the crust: Preheat the oven to 350 degrees. Grease a 10-inch springform pan and set aside. In a small bowl mix the graham cracker crumbs, orange rind, and butter. Press in the bottom of the springform pan. Bake for 8 minutes. Remove from the oven and cool while preparing the filling.

To prepare the filling: Reduce the oven temperature to 300 degrees. Place the softened cream cheese in the bowl of your electric mixer and whip for 2 minutes. Blend in the cheddar cheese. In a small bowl mix the flour and sugar. With the mixer still running gradually add the flour mixture. Add the eggs one at a time, beating until smooth. Add the orange juice, heavy cream, orange rind, and vanilla. Continue to mix until ingredients are incorporated. Pour into the prepared crust and bake for 1 ½ hours. Test the center for firmness. Cool. Refrigerate for at least 2 hours before serving. Serve with orange sauce.

To make the orange sauce: In a medium saucepan mix the sugar, flour, and salt. Add the orange rind, orange juice, lemon juice, and egg yolks. Place over low heat and stir until thick. Add the butter, stir, and set aside to cool. Whip the heavy cream until soft peaks form. Fold the whipped cream into the orange sauce and refrigerate for at least 2 hours. Serve on top of the cake slices.

Makes 12 to 14 servings.

Black and Gold Chocolate Chip Cake

Living right outside of Nashville, I have been to many tailgate parties at Vanderbilt and served this cake in support of the Commodores.

Cake:
- 1 (18.25-ounce) box butter cake mix
- 1 (3-ounce) box vanilla instant pudding
- ½ cup butter, softened
- 4 large eggs
- ½ cup milk
- ½ cup vegetable oil
- 1 cup sour cream
- 1 (10-ounce) package semisweet chocolate chips
- 2 cups chopped pecans

Icing:
- 1 (8-ounce) package cream cheese, softened
- 3 ½ cups powdered sugar
- 1 ½ teaspoons vanilla
- ⅓ cup chopped pecans
- ⅓ cup flaked coconut

To make the cake: Preheat the oven to 350 degrees. Grease and flour a 10-inch Bundt pan. Set aside. In a large bowl add the cake mix, instant pudding, butter, eggs, and milk and mix well. Add the oil and sour cream, stirring to combine. Fold in the chocolate chips and pecans. Pour into the prepared Bundt pan. Bake for 1 hour. Remove from the oven and allow to cool 10 minutes before removing from the pan. Place on cake plate and let cool completely before icing.
To make the icing: In a large bowl mix the cream cheese and sugar until well blended. Add the vanilla. Spread on the top and sides of the cooled cake. Sprinkle the pecans and coconut over the top.

Makes 16 servings.

My Blueberry Heaven Pie

Kentucky, Duke, MTSU, UVA, and, of course, the Tennessee Titans fans will be in heaven when you take this to a tailgate party.

Crust:
- 2 cups graham cracker crumbs
- ½ cup powdered sugar
- 1 cup chopped pecans
- ½ cup unsalted butter, melted

Filling:
- 1 cup sugar
- 1 (8-ounce) package cream cheese
- 2 large eggs, slightly beaten
- 1 tablespoon lemon juice
- 1 (20-ounce) can blueberry pie filling

Topping:
- 2 cups heavy whipping cream
- ¼ cup powdered sugar

To make the crust: Preheat the oven to 350 degrees. In a medium bowl combine the graham cracker crumbs, powdered sugar, and pecans. Add the melted butter and mix well. Spread the mixture in a 13 x 9-inch baking dish and set aside while you prepare the filling.

To make the filling: In a medium bowl, mix the sugar and cream cheese. Add the eggs and lemon juice and mix well. Spread over the crust. Bake for 20 minutes. Let cool and top with the blueberry pie filling.

To prepare the topping: In a small to medium bowl whip the heavy cream and sugar with an electric mixer until stiff peaks form. Spread on top of the pie and serve.

Makes 16 servings.

♥ CHAPTER 7 ♥

PARTY
TIME

IT'S MY PARTY AND I'LL FRY IF I WANT TO

Honey was delighted when her sister called to see if she would cohost an engagement party for her niece. "I'd love to," she said. "I can bring my award-winning petits fours."

After Honey won a baking contest put on by the regional home economics council, she became convinced she was the only person in the entire South who had mastered those tiny confections. And when she was interviewed by the local cable access station for its series on "The Lost Art of Icing," she became even more unbearable, or so her sister said.

"That won't be necessary," said her sister, interrupting Honey just as she always had during their childhood years when they shared a bedroom. "We've got a system in place." The "we" in this case referred to ten mothers who had made a pact with one another to throw an expertly coordinated engagement party for each others' daughters when the time came.

"When one of our daughters gets engaged we divide up the responsibilities for a party. We've done it several times now, so we've got it down to a science. It's just that one of the women can't help this time."

When a young man popped the question to one of their daughters, this select group of women leapt into action, pulling out their calendars and their to-do lists, setting in motion a social machine to rival the efforts of Martha Stewart and Paula Deen combined. Before you knew it, the party was planned, invitations were mailed, and a piano player was hired. In return for hosting the other girls' parties, your own precious girl would get a party when her time came. Now it was Honey's niece's turn.

Honey, never all that lucky in love herself, desperately wanted to ask her sister what would happen if one of the girls never met Mr. Right, but instead simply said, "I'm flattered."

"Great," said Honey's sister. "Make sure you're on time. And don't wear that floral number that makes you look like Aunt Tilda's tea cozy."

It wasn't long before Honey started receiving e-mails from the women about the party. And although it irked her, Honey had to admit these women were good. They knew which Saturday was out because of football games for the current season and the next; how many pounds of Parmesan walnuts you needed for seventy-five people; what ratio of sparkling water to juice is required for punch that will last the night; and where to get the best deals on fresh flowers.

♥

Honey had left her hometown and moved to the northern part of the state in order to see the world, so she didn't know her sister's friends. And she certainly didn't know what "science" had to do with party food. But Honey has never been the troublemaker in the family—that distinction falls to the third sister, Jane Ellen—and she adored her niece, so she told herself it wouldn't be that bad. Honey had long ago learned to look on the bright side whenever possible.

Honey had also learned that sometimes there's not enough good attitude in the world to make the glass half full. After driving 117 miles on a two-lane highway she arrived in town the night of the party and secured the last room at the Strawberry Acres B&B. (She had forgotten there was a race at the nearby speedway.) Tired, but excited to celebrate her niece's engagement, she hurried over to the event only to find out that the women had assigned her to kitchen duty.

"It's tradition," said the ringleader, a woman named Constance who wore a monogrammed, grosgrain ribbon headband that could only be classified as unseemly on a woman her age, "that the newest hostess handles the food table and the dishes. Here's an apron. You'll need to hand wash those punch cups; they belonged to my grandmother."

Honey had a few questions for Constance, such as "Is anyone going to be helping me?" and "How do you live with yourself?" and "Did you really mean to wear those shoes with that dress?" but Constance left the kitchen with such speed and enthusiasm that Honey was not able to approach her in a timely fashion. As the door swung shut, Honey tried not to think about what she'd like to do with those punch cups. Her mother had raised her right, after all, so she turned her attention to the bounty laid out on the granite countertops: bacon-wrapped dates and salmon pinwheels, crab dip, and teacakes. Chicken skewers for dipping and small pastry shells filled with lemon curd, which Honey would have topped with fresh blueberries if she had been assigned to lemon tart duty.

Because no one was paying attention to Honey anyway, it wasn't hard for her to slip out to her car and grab the box of petits fours she had brought along, "just in case." She began nestling her tiny works of art, each one a testament to what a woman can do with sugar and flour if she puts her mind to it, among the other sweets. If she placed the tray just so, the edible pearls on top of her petits fours glistened like icicles in the light of the chandelier, an overdone number with way too many faux crystals for Honey's taste.

When her sister came up behind her at the sink an hour or so later, she caught Honey off guard.

"I know you brought those darned petits fours of yours," she said, tapping her right foot like she did when she got worked up. "And now you've gone and done it."

As Honey turned to face her accuser, she dropped the punch cup she was soaping.

"You better clean that up before Constance finds out," said her sister. "Anyway, Sally Virginia wants your petits fours for her daughter's party next month. They expect at least 150 people, and her daughter's colors are robin's egg blue and pale yellow."

"Okay," said Honey, smiling just a bit, but not so much as to appear smug. She grabbed a broom and began sweeping up the amber shards of glass that had settled around her sister's maroon Aigner pumps. "No problem."

Honey wrapped the broken glass in paper towels and stuck it in her handbag. She would get rid of the evidence on her way out of town, maybe use the dumpster behind the inn. Honey was as honest as the day is long, but she didn't see the need to bother Constance with the news that she had broken one of her grandmother's beloved punch cups. Honey wasn't convinced they were the real deal anyway, as they looked nothing like the pressed glass that had been handed down in her family. She finished cleaning the kitchen before she slipped out the back door, content to return to the Strawberry Acres B&B and sleep the sleep of the vindicated, her reputation for making the best petits fours in the state intact, and her sister owing her big time.

Slush Punch

This travels well since it needs to thaw a couple of hours before serving.

- 3 ½ cups sugar
- 6 cups water
- 2 (3-ounce) packages peach gelatin, or your favorite flavor
- 1 (46-ounce) can pineapple juice
- 1 quart fresh orange juice
- ⅔ cup fresh lemon juice
- 1 (64-ounce) bottle ginger ale

In a large saucepan combine the sugar and water. Bring to a boil and simmer for 3 minutes. Remove from the heat and stir in the gelatin to dissolve. Pour into a 2-gallon container. Add the pineapple juice, orange juice, and lemon juice and mix well. Ladle into wide-topped freezer containers, leaving 2 inches of headspace. Cover tightly and freeze.

To serve: Thaw at room temperature for 2 hours. Place the slush in a punch bowl and stir with a fork to break up the ice chunks. Add ginger ale and serve.

Makes 1 ½ gallons or 48 (4-ounce) servings.

Cajun Green Beans

The addition of the Creole seasoning turns this dish into something magical.

- 1 (32-ounce) package frozen cut green beans
- 1 ½ tablespoons Creole seasoning
- ¼ teaspoon red pepper flakes
- ⅓ cup chopped red bell pepper
- 6 slices peppered bacon, diced
- ⅓ cup chopped onion
- 2 tablespoons chopped celery
- 2 tablespoons chopped green bell pepper
- ½ cup butter

Preheat the oven to 375 degrees. Place the green beans in a 13 x 9-inch baking dish and sprinkle with the Creole seasoning. Add the red pepper flakes, red bell pepper, bacon, onion, celery, and green bell pepper. Dot the top with the butter. Bake for about 45 minutes or until the beans are tender, stirring every 15 minutes.

Makes 12 servings.

Miniature BLTs

These are good at every kind of party you can imagine.

- 8 slices white bread
- 1 cup mayonnaise
- 4 slices bacon, cooked and crumbled
- 2 teaspoons lemon juice
- 1 tablespoon finely chopped parsley
- 8 small Roma tomatoes, each cut into 4 slices

Cut rounds from the bread slices using a 1 ¾-inch biscuit cutter. You should be able to get 4 rounds per slice of bread. In a small mixing bowl combine the mayonnaise, bacon, lemon juice, and parsley. Spread the mayonnaise mixture on the bread rounds and top with a tomato slice.

Makes 32 rounds.

Refrigerator Rolls

This is a different spin on the traditional yeast roll.

⅓ cup lukewarm water
2 (¼-ounce) envelopes active dry yeast
1 teaspoon sugar
1 cup boiling water
1 cup vegetable shortening
⅔ cup sugar
1 teaspoon salt
2 large eggs, slightly beaten
1 cup cold water
6 cups all-purpose flour, divided
2 tablespoons oil, divided
¼ cup melted butter

Place the lukewarm water in a small bowl. Add the yeast and 1 teaspoon of sugar and stir. Let sit for 3 to 4 minutes or until the yeast begins to bubble. Set aside. In the bowl of an electric mixer, pour 1 cup boiling water and add the shortening, ¾ cup of sugar, and salt, mixing well. In a small bowl combine the eggs and cold water. Add the egg mixture to the shortening mixture. Add 2 cups of the flour to the shortening mixture and mix to form a soft dough. Add the reserved yeast mixture and continue to beat, gradually adding the remaining 4 cups flour. Beat until the dough leaves the sides of the bowl.

Oil the top of the dough with one tablespoon of the oil and cover with a cloth. Let rise at room temperature for about 2 hours or until the dough doubles in size. Punch the dough down to remove the air and brush the remaining 1 tablespoon oil on top. Place in the refrigerator overnight.

The next day, roll to ½-inch thick and cut as biscuits or other shapes. Place on a greased baking sheet. Brush the tops with the melted butter and let the dough rise for 2 to 3 hours before baking. Preheat the oven to 400 degrees. Bake for 12 to 15 minutes.

Makes 3 dozen rolls.

Addictive Parmesan Walnuts

Eat just one. I dare you.

- 4 cups English walnut halves
- 2 tablespoons butter, melted
- ½ teaspoon salt
- ½ cup grated Parmesan cheese

Preheat the oven to 325 degrees. Spread the walnuts on a 15 x 10-inch baking sheet, and bake for 8 to 10 minutes. In a small bowl combine the butter, salt, and Parmesan cheese. Sprinkle over the walnuts and stir to coat. Return to the oven and bake for 3 minutes.

Pour the walnuts on a large piece of parchment paper to cool. Store in a covered container.

Makes 4 cups.

Five Vegetable Slaw

Pretty and delicious too!

- 1 medium head cabbage, shredded (6 to 8 cups)
- 3 medium tomatoes, diced
- 1 large cucumber, peeled, seeded, and diced
- 1 large green bell pepper, seeded and diced
- 1 cup diced red onion
- ½ cup mayonnaise
- ½ cup white vinegar
- ¼ cup sugar
- ¼ teaspoon salt
- ¼ teaspoon black pepper

In a large bowl combine the cabbage, tomatoes, cucumber, green bell pepper, and onion.

In a medium bowl stir the mayonnaise, vinegar, sugar, salt, and pepper until smooth. Pour the sauce over the vegetables and stir to mix. Cover and refrigerate for at least two 2 hours before serving.

Makes 12 servings.

Marinated Broccoli, Cauliflower, and Tomatoes

This is a pretty, colorful party dish.

- 1 cup apple cider vinegar
- 2 teaspoons dried dill
- 1 tablespoon sugar
- 2 teaspoons seasoned salt
- 1 teaspoon garlic salt
- 1 teaspoon salt
- 1 teaspoon black pepper
- 1 ¼ cups vegetable oil
- 4 cups broccoli florets
- 4 cups cauliflower florets
- 2 cups grape tomatoes
- Toothpicks for serving

In a nonreactive bowl add the vinegar, dill, sugar, seasoned salt, garlic salt, salt, and black pepper. Whisk in the oil to make the dressing. Set aside while you prepare the vegetables. In a large bowl add the broccoli, cauliflower, and tomatoes. Pour the dressing over the vegetables and toss gently. Cover and refrigerate for 4 to 6 hours before serving.

To serve: Drain and place in a serving bowl. Serve with toothpicks.

Makes 16 servings.

Beef Tenderloin with Blue Cheese Topping

Personally I think beef tenderloin served with rolls is the perfect party food. But this is also excellent served as the main course at dinner.

Tenderloin:

- 1 (3- to 4-pound) beef tenderloin, trimmed
- ¼ cup olive oil
- 1 tablespoon coarse salt
- 2 teaspoons black pepper

Blue cheese topping:

- 1 clove garlic
- 1 tablespoon Worcestershire sauce
- 4 ounces blue cheese, crumbled
- ½ cup butter, softened

To make the tenderloin: Preheat the oven to 450 degrees. Grease a 13 x 9-inch baking dish. Place the tenderloin in the baking dish and brush with the olive oil. Cover with the salt and pepper. Bake in the oven for 30 minutes or until the meat thermometer registers 130 degrees (for rare). While the meat is cooking prepare the blue cheese topping.

To make the blue cheese topping: In a small bowl mash the garlic and Worcestershire sauce. Add the blue cheese and butter and blend well. Spread the mixture on top of the cooked tenderloin and cover loosely with foil. Let rest 20 minutes before slicing.

Makes 10 servings.

Grilled Chicken and Pineapple Kabobs

When you take this to a party, be sure to stick it in the oven to warm before serving.

½	cup soy sauce
½	cup pineapple juice
¼	cup canola oil
1	tablespoon firmly packed brown sugar
½	teaspoon garlic powder
1 ½	teaspoons ground ginger
1	teaspoon dry mustard
½	teaspoon black pepper
4	(5- to 6-ounce) boneless chicken breasts cut into 1-inch cubes
12	wooden skewers for grilling
1	(20-ounce) can pineapple chunks, drained
1	large green bell pepper, cut into 1-inch cubes

In a small saucepan combine the soy sauce, pineapple juice, canola oil, brown sugar, garlic powder, ginger, mustard, and black pepper. Place over medium heat and bring to a boil. Reduce heat and simmer for 5 minutes. Set aside to cool. Place the chicken pieces in a shallow dish. Pour the marinade over the chicken and refrigerate for 2 hours.

Meanwhile, soak the wooden skewers in water for at least 30 minutes. To assemble the skewers alternate the chicken, pineapple chunks, and cubes of green pepper. Grill for 15 minutes, turning frequently.

Makes 12 servings.

Fresh from the Garden Tomato Pie

I teach several cooking classes every year. This recipe is always a class favorite.

- 3 medium-size tomatoes, peeled and thickly sliced
- 1 (9-inch) piecrust, unbaked
- ½ teaspoon salt
- ½ teaspoon black pepper
- ½ teaspoon dried basil
- ¼ cup finely chopped chives
- ½ cup mayonnaise
- 1 ½ cups shredded cheddar cheese
  Parchment paper

Prehcat the oven to 400 degrees. Place the tomato slices in the unbaked piecrust and season with the salt, pepper, and basil. Sprinkle with the chives. In a small bowl add the mayonnaise and cheddar cheese, stirring to mix well. Put the cheese mixture on a square of parchment paper. Cover with another square of parchment paper and flatten to a 9-inch round. Remove the top parchment paper. Turn the cheese-mayonnaise mixture upside down over the tomatoes, making sure the cheese goes to the edge of the pie. Bake for 30 minutes. Serve warm.

Makes 6 to 8 servings.

Strawberry Stuffed Strawberries

I can't think of a better party food.

- 26 large strawberries, washed
- 4 ounces cream cheese, softened
- 3 tablespoons finely chopped walnuts
- 2 tablespoons powdered sugar
- 2 teaspoons orange juice

Finely chop 2 strawberries and set aside. Turn each of the remaining 24 strawberries on their stem and carefully slice each one into four wedges, making sure that each wedge is still connected to the stem. In a small bowl beat the cream cheese until fluffy. Stir in the reserved chopped strawberries, walnuts, powdered sugar, and orange juice. Spoon the mixture into a pastry bag fitted with a star tip, and pipe evenly into the strawberry cups.

Makes 24 strawberry cups.

Pineapple Cheese Salad

This is the type of salad that Southern ladies have been serving on a bed of lettuce leaves for generations.

- 1 (20-ounce) can crushed pineapple
- 1 (3-ounce) package lemon gelatin
- 2 teaspoons lemon juice
- 1 cup chopped pecans
- 1 cup shredded cheddar cheese
- 1 cup heavy whipping cream

Drain the pineapple juice into a small saucepan and set the pineapple aside. Cook the juice over medium heat and add the gelatin, stirring to dissolve. Add the lemon juice, stir, and set aside to cool at room temperature. When cool, add the pineapple, pecans, and cheese, stirring to combine. Place in the refrigerator for 45 minutes to an hour or until mixture begins to congeal.

In a small bowl beat the heavy cream with an electric mixer until it forms soft peaks. Fold the whipped cream into the gelatin mixture and place in a ring mold or glass serving dish. Refrigerate for an additional 2 hours or until firm.

Makes 8 to 10 servings.

Petite Party Burgers

I made these for the first time in 1989 for an art gallery opening and they were a huge hit. I've made thousands since.

1 ½	pounds ground beef
1	teaspoon salt
1	teaspoon black pepper
½	cup finely chopped onion
	Paper towels
1	(20-count) package party rolls
⅓	cup mustard
20	dill pickle slices

Preheat the oven to 450 degrees. Flatten the ground beef on a 13 x 9 x 1-inch cookie sheet to ¼-inch thickness. Season the beef with the salt and pepper. Press the chopped onion into the meat. Bake for 10 to 15 minutes. Remove from the oven and using a spatula, place the beef on paper towels to absorb the grease. Cut the beef into 20 little burgers, according to the size and shape of the rolls.

Split the party rolls in half with a serrated knife. Spread the mustard on one side of the rolls. Top with the meat. Cover with pickle slices. Top with the remaining halves of the rolls. Wrap in aluminum foil and place in the refrigerator until time to reheat.

Makes 20 little burgers.

"Just Chill" Ham and Pasta Salad

While a great party appetizer, this is actually hearty enough to serve as a main course.

Pasta salad:
- 1 (8-ounce) package elbow macaroni
- ½ cup chopped red bell pepper
- ¼ cup finely chopped celery
- ¼ cup finely chopped onion
- 1 cup sliced fresh mushrooms
- 1 cup broccoli, cooked and chopped
- 2 boiled eggs, chopped
- 1 cup shredded cheddar cheese
- 2 cups diced cooked ham
- 1 cup diced tomatoes

Dressing:
- ¼ cup red wine vinegar
- ½ cup sour cream
- ½ cup mayonnaise

To make the pasta salad: Cook the macaroni according to package directions, drain and rinse with cold water. In a large bowl add the macaroni, red bell pepper, celery, onion, mushrooms, broccoli, eggs, cheese, ham, and tomatoes. Mix gently.

To make the dressing: In a small bowl combine the vinegar, sour cream, and mayonnaise. Mix well and pour over the pasta salad. Toss. Let chill for 2 hours before serving.

Makes 8 to 10 servings.

Miniature Cherry Cheesecakes

You might think that one of these for each of your guests would be enough, but trust me, it won't be.

- ½ cup graham cracker crumbs
- 2 tablespoons butter, melted
- 1 (8-ounce) package cream cheese, softened
- ¼ cup sugar
- 1 large egg, slightly beaten
- ½ teaspoon vanilla extract
- 1 (20-ounce) can cherry pie filling

Preheat the oven to 350 degrees. Line 2 mini-muffin tins with paper liners. In a small bowl mix the graham cracker crumbs and butter together. Spoon 1 teaspoon of the crumbs into each muffin cup and press down. In a medium bowl beat the cream cheese, sugar, egg, and vanilla until well mixed. Spoon the cream cheese mixture onto the crumbs and bake for 10 minutes. Place one teaspoon of cherry pie filling on top of each miniature cheesecake. Chill until serving time.

Makes 24 miniature cheesecakes.

NOTE: People will want more than one, so plan accordingly.

Tess's Peanut Butter Fudge

My sister Tess makes this fudge every Christmas and delivers it all over our small town as gifts. She takes it to the bank, to the place she gets her car worked on, and to personal friends. It's a much-loved tradition in Charlotte, Tennessee. My children look forward to eating this every year.

- ½ cup milk
- 2 cups sugar
- 2 tablespoons corn syrup
- 1 tablespoon butter
- ½ cup peanut butter, creamy or crunchy
- 1 teaspoon vanilla extract

In a medium saucepan combine the milk, sugar, and corn syrup. Bring the mixture to a boil over low heat and let boil for 3 minutes. Remove from the heat and add the butter, peanut butter, and vanilla. Beat with a wooden spoon until the mixture begins to thicken. Pour into a buttered 9-inch-square dish. When cool cut into squares.

Makes 3 dozen squares.

Homemade Chocolate Drop Candy

This is great to have on hand for the holidays to serve when unexpected guests drop by.

- 1 (7-ounce) jar marshmallow cream
- 1 ½ pounds (24 ounces) Hershey's kisses, unwrapped
- 5 cups sugar
- 1 (13-ounce) can evaporated milk
- ½ cup butter
- 6 cups pecan halves

In a large bowl mix the marshmallow cream and Hershey's kisses. Set aside. In a large saucepan combine the sugar, milk, and butter. Bring to a boil over medium heat. Stir and continue to cook for 8 minutes. Pour the sugar mixture over the marshmallow and chocolate mixture and stir until the chocolate is melted. Fold in the pecans. Drop by teaspoons onto waxed paper. Allow the candy to harden.

Makes 8 to 10 dozen candies.

NOTE: Store in an airtight container.

Corn Blueberry Muffins

You probably wouldn't think of serving a regular blueberry muffin except at breakfast or brunch. But this muffin is at home on your table morning, noon, or night.

- 1 cup cornmeal
- 1 cup all-purpose flour
- ½ cup sugar
- 2 ½ teaspoons baking powder
- ¼ teaspoon salt
- 1 cup buttermilk
- 6 tablespoons butter, melted
- 1 large egg, slightly beaten
- 1 ½ cups blueberries

Preheat the oven to 400 degrees. Prepare a 12-cup muffin pan with paper liners and set aside. In a large mixing bowl sift together the cornmeal, flour, sugar, baking powder, and salt. Add the buttermilk, melted butter, and egg. Stir until just combined and fold in the blueberries. Fill the prepared muffin cups ⅔ full and bake for 20 minutes.

Makes 12 servings.

Summer Fresh Peach Pie (page 165)

♥ CHAPTER 8 ♥

BOOK CLUBS

TURN THE PAGE
AND PASS THE MUFFINS

Ella was tickled pink when Rose called to invite her to join the Luckettville Learned Ladies Society.

"It can take years for someone to leave the group," Ella told me, flush with pride over her new status. "I can't believe my good fortune."

Now, most folks wouldn't call the death of Mrs. Winters good fortune, unless it was Mrs. Winters herself, seeing that she was about a hundred and hadn't heard a word that was said by any of the Luckettville Learned Ladies for at least three years. I feel sure Ella didn't mean any disrespect. She was simply a woman who knew what she wanted, and she had wanted a chair around Rose's oak dining room table on Wednesday mornings from nine to eleven ever since her youngest left for basic training.

"God knows I love my husband," Ella would say. "But with just the two of us at home now, a little Leon goes a long way. I've signed up for extra volunteer shifts at the community center, but I still need an excuse to get out of the house on Wednesdays."

♥

Early on the morning of her Luckettville Learned Ladies Society debut, Ella called her daughter, Anna Fair, to find out what might be expected of her. Anna Fair had a reputation for keeping up with cultural trends and introducing them to her friends long before the rest of the town caught on. Why, just last month she brought sushi to dinner on the grounds at Mt. Moriah Last Chance Chapel, where she was baptized, confirmed, and now teaches Sunday school to the first graders. Granted, Anna Fair is the only person in the congregation who's ever tried to pass off raw fish wrapped in seaweed as something everyone "simply had to try once," but her mother loved her daughter for being willing to take such a risk. Ella had never been much of a maverick herself.

So anyway, Anna Fair started her own book group a year or so ago called the "Luckettville Liberated Literary Coalition," and it has the distinction of being the only club in Luckettville devoted solely to books by female authors. Ella hoped her daughter's experience with that group might guide her somewhat in what to expect at Rose's house.

"After we catch up with one another," said Anna Fair, "you know—jobs, vacations, blog postings—then we open the . . ."

"Open the what?" asked Ella.

Suddenly Anna Fair sounded very far away even though she lived four doors down in her grandmother's old Colonial. "We drink a little wine, Mother. There, I've said it. But we never have more than one glass apiece. I promise."

"Deliver me," said Ella. "Surely you don't think that goes on at the Luckettville Learned Ladies Society, do you?" Ella did not believe this was the time to confess to her daughter that she herself indulges in a glass of fermented grape juice on occasion, but only because Doc Easton assures her it has medicinal properties. In moderation, of course.

"Who knows?" said Anna Fair. "They're so secretive we wouldn't know if they really read tarot cards and shoot dice. I've always thought that Mrs. Hendricks seemed a little—"

"Anna Fair Stallings," said Ella. "Watch your mouth, young lady."

Even at twenty-eight years old, and as independent and forward thinking as Anna Fair was, she knew there were still times when only two words would do.

"Yes, ma'am," she said.

After she hung up the phone, Ella started to panic. She had spent hours preparing food to take to the Luckettville Learned Ladies Society, but it hadn't occurred to her to worry about something to drink. And now there wasn't enough time to make a gallon of fruit tea. If she'd thought of it, she would have bought a jar of maraschino cherries and mixed a batch of Shirley Temples for everyone. My how she had loved those drinks ever since her daddy took her to the Rotary Club's father-daughter dinner in junior high. It was too late now. Anyway, for all Ella knew, she had pored over that long book and prepared all this food for a bunch of culturally depraved heathens masquerading as well-read women of faith.

In the end, Ella needn't have worried. When she arrived on Rose's doorstep with her copy of *The History of Luckettville: The Early Years*, cluttered with notations in the margins and little slips of paper jutting out from each chapter as if she were a seasoned professor teaching Faulkner at the college, it was obvious the other women were impressed. And the fact that Ella brought food even though the newest inductee doesn't have to until her second meeting guaranteed her a "lifetime member in good standing" distinction in the Luckettville Learned Ladies Society right then and there. Ella had come bearing her trusted standbys: peppermint brownies with milk-chocolate icing, cream cheese sandwiches cut into triangles, and broccoli florets with a side of her bacon-tomato dip.

Ella would love to tell you what all went on around Rose's dining room table that morning, but the guiding principles outlined on page three of the *Luckettville Learned Ladies Society Handbook* will not allow her to reveal even one word. You'll just have to wait until you get your own invitation to join, which, as luck would have it, could come any day now. According to Ella, Miss Hibernia is not looking too good.

Cream of Strawberry Punch

This is a beautiful drink that will be popular at a meeting, a shower, or a tea.

- 1 (46-ounce) can pineapple juice, chilled
- 2 ¼ cups water
- 6 ounces frozen pink lemonade concentrate, thawed and undiluted
- 1 (64-ounce) bottle ginger ale, chilled
- 1 quart strawberry ice cream

In a large punchbowl combine the pineapple juice, water, lemonade, and ginger ale. Spoon the ice cream in the bowl, stirring gently to mix.

Makes 1 ¾ gallons.

Summer Fresh Peach Pie

The cream cheese crust and the combination of fresh peaches make this dessert a winner.

- ¼ cup powdered sugar
- 4 ounces cream cheese
- 1 (9-inch) baked piecrust
- 3 tablespoons peach gelatin
- 3 tablespoons cornstarch
- 1 cup plus 2 tablespoons sugar, divided
- 1 cup water
- 4 to 5 medium-size fresh peaches, peeled and sliced
- 1 cup heavy whipping cream

In a small bowl mix the powdered sugar and cream cheese together. Stir to mix well and spread over the baked and cooled piecrust. In a small saucepan mix the peach gelatin, cornstarch, 1 cup of the sugar, and water together over medium heat. Bring to a boil, stirring constantly. Cook approximately 3 minutes until the mixture becomes transparent and thick. Remove from the heat and cool.

When you are ready to assemble the pie, place the sliced peaches over the cream cheese mixture. Pour the peach gelatin filling over the sliced peaches. Using an electric mixer whip the heavy whipping cream and the remaining 2 tablespoons sugar until soft peaks form. Spread on top of the pie. Refrigerate for 1 hour before serving.

Makes 1 pie or 6 to 8 servings.

English Pea Salad

This is a great springtime salad.

1   (16-ounce) can tiny English peas
2   medium tomatoes, peeled and diced
1   cup finely diced onion
⅓   cup mayonnaise
½   teaspoon salt
½   teaspoon black pepper

Rinse and drain the peas and place in a medium bowl. Add the tomatoes, onion, mayonnaise, salt, and pepper. Mix well. Chill for 2 hours before serving.

Makes 8 servings.

Peach Pecan Muffins

I love peaches all year long. This recipe allows you to enjoy the taste of peaches during those long months when fresh Southern peaches aren't available.

½   cup butter, softened
¾   cup sugar
1   large egg, slightly beaten
1   teaspoon vanilla extract
½   cup sour cream
1 ½   cups all-purpose flour
1 ½   teaspoons baking powder
⅛   teaspoon salt
1   cup chopped frozen peaches
1   cup chopped pecans

Preheat the oven to 400 degrees. Prepare one 12-cup muffin tin by placing paper liners in each cup. Set aside. In a large bowl cream the butter and sugar together until well mixed. Add the egg, vanilla, and sour cream, mixing well. In a medium bowl combine the flour, baking powder, and salt. Blend the flour mixture into the sour cream mixture. Fold in the peaches and pecans and stir until just moistened. Fill the prepared muffin cups ⅔ full with the batter. Bake for 20 minutes.

Makes 12 servings.

Angel Biscuits

These make the perfect addition to a meeting of any kind, especially when they're stuffed with ham. The dough can be refrigerated for up to four days.

- 1 package active dry yeast
- 2 tablespoons warm water
- ¼ cup sugar
- 5 cups all-purpose flour
- 1 teaspoon baking soda
- 3 teaspoons baking powder
- 1 teaspoon salt
- 1 cup vegetable shortening
- 2 cups buttermilk

Preheat the oven to 400 degrees. Grease a large baking sheet and set aside. In a small bowl dissolve the yeast in the warm water and set aside while you prepare the dry ingredients. In a large bowl sift together the sugar, flour, baking soda, baking powder, and salt. Add the shortening, using your fingers or a pastry blender to combine. Add the yeast mixture and buttermilk to the dry mixture. Knead enough to hold together.

Turn out onto a lightly floured board, adding more flour if necessary to roll. Roll to about ½-inch thick. Cut with a 2 ½-inch biscuit cutter and place on the prepared baking sheet. Bake for 20 minutes.

Makes 3 dozen angel biscuits.

Banana Bread with Ambrosia Topping

I personally think banana bread is close to perfect. This ambrosia topping gets it all the way there.

Banana bread:
- 2 cups all-purpose flour
- 1 teaspoon baking soda
- ¼ teaspoon salt
- ½ cup butter, softened
- 1 cup sugar
- 2 large eggs
- 1 teaspoon vanilla extract
- 3 large bananas, mashed
- 1 cup chopped pecans

Ambrosia topping:
- 1 (8-ounce) package cream cheese, softened
- 1 (8-ounce) can crushed pineapple, drained
- ⅓ cup flaked coconut, toasted
- ⅓ cup toasted almonds, chopped
- 1 tablespoon sugar

To make the banana bread: Preheat the oven to 325 degrees. Grease a 9 x 5 x 3-inch loaf pan. In a small bowl sift together the flour, baking soda, and salt and set aside. In a medium bowl cream the butter and sugar. Add the eggs one at a time, beating well after each addition. Add the vanilla and bananas and mix well. Fold in the dry ingredients and the pecans. Pour into the prepared loaf pan. Bake for 50 to 60 minutes, or until a toothpick inserted in the center comes out clean. Remove from the pan to cool.

To make the ambrosia topping: In a medium bowl beat the cream cheese until smooth. Add the pineapple, coconut, almonds, and sugar. Stir to mix well.

To serve: Spread the ambrosia on the sliced banana bread.

Makes 12 servings.

Cranberry Apple Bake

This is a tradition at our home for Christmas and Thanksgiving. But don't forget this recipe when you are planning a brunch menu at any time of the year.

Fruit:
- 3 cups peeled, cored, and chopped apples
- 2 cups fresh cranberries
- 2 tablespoons all-purpose flour
- 1 cup sugar

Topping:
- 1 cup quick-cooking oats
- ½ teaspoon cinnamon
- ¾ cup chopped pecans
- ½ cup firmly packed brown sugar
- ½ cup all-purpose flour
- ½ cup butter, melted

Preheat the oven to 350 degrees.

To prepare the fruit: Grease a 13 x 9-inch baking dish. In a medium bowl toss the apples, cranberries, flour, and sugar and place in the prepared dish.

To prepare the topping: In a medium bowl add the oats, cinnamon, pecans, sugar, flour, and melted butter. Mix well and sprinkle over the cranberry-apple mixture. Bake uncovered for 45 minutes.

Makes 8 to 10 servings.

Sour Cream Drop Biscuits

Sometimes even the best Southern cook doesn't want to pull out the rolling pin and make a mess in the kitchen. These are a delicious solution.

- 2 cups baking mix
- ½ cup butter, melted
- 1 cup sour cream

Preheat the oven to 350 degrees. Grease one 12-cup muffin tin and set aside. In a medium bowl add the baking mix, melted butter, and sour cream. Mix all the ingredients until just moistened. Fill the prepared muffin cups ⅔ full. Bake for 15 to 20 minutes or until golden brown.

Makes 1 dozen biscuits.

Bacon Tomato Dip

This is wonderful with carrot or celery sticks, but you could also serve with it with small crackers.

- 10 slices bacon, cooked and diced
- 2 large tomatoes, peeled and diced
- 1 cup mayonnaise
- 2 teaspoons Dijon mustard
- 2 tablespoons minced green onions
- 2 tablespoons finely chopped parsley
- ¼ teaspoon Tabasco sauce

In a large bowl combine the diced bacon, tomatoes, mayonnaise, mustard, onions, parsley, and Tabasco sauce. Stir to mix well.

Makes 12 servings.

NOTE: This may be prepared a day ahead and kept refrigerated.

Watercress Sandwiches

Wherever two or more Southern ladies are gathered together, you are almost certain to find a watercress sandwich.

- 16 slices thin white bread
- ⅓ cup watercress
- 2 tablespoons parsley
- ½ cup butter
- 4 ounces cream cheese
- ¼ teaspoon black pepper
- 1 tablespoon minced chives
- 1 teaspoon lemon juice

Remove the crusts from the bread. Chop the watercress and parsley together until fine. In a medium bowl blend the butter, cream cheese, chopped watercress, and parsley. Add the black pepper, chives, and lemon juice. Stir to mix well.

To serve: Spread on one side of eight slices of bread and place the other eight slices on top. Cut into quarters.

Makes 32 servings.

Tuna Salad with Apples and Craisins

The ladies in my cooking classes rave about this easy and delicious dish. If you're not a fan of Craisins, you can substitute grapes, but I like the nice tart kick they provide.

2   (6-ounce) cans tuna packed in water, drained and rinsed
¾   cup Craisins
½   cup chopped pecans
¼   cup finely diced sweet pickles
1   cup shredded Monterey Jack or cheddar cheese
1   cup peeled and finely diced apples
½   cup mayonnaise

In a medium bowl combine the tuna, Craisins, pecans, sweet pickles, cheese, and apples. Stir to mix well. Fold in the mayonnaise. Add more mayonnaise if you like your tuna a little moister. Store in the refrigerator.

Makes 6 to 8 sandwiches.

Bacon and Cheese Grits

This dish is good for any meal of the day.

1   cup regular grits, cooked according to package directions
½   cup butter
2   cups shredded mild cheddar cheese, divided
¼   teaspoon garlic salt (optional)
3   large eggs, well beaten
⅔   cup milk
6   slices bacon, cooked and crumbled

Preheat the oven to 350 degrees. Grease a 2-quart baking dish and set aside. While the grits are hot, add the butter and 1 ½ cups of the cheese. Stir until the cheese melts. Cool slightly and then add the garlic salt, eggs, and milk. Pour into the prepared dish. Top with the remaining ½ cup cheddar cheese. Bake for 35 to 40 minutes.

To serve: Top with the cooked, crumbled bacon and serve immediately.

Makes 8 to 10 servings.

Bacon, Egg, and Cheese Casserole

My daughter serves this at her home every Christmas morning. The beauty of this recipe is that you do the majority of the work the day ahead.

- ¼ cup butter, melted
- 6 slices white bread, cubed
- 2 ½ cups shredded cheddar cheese, divided
- 8 large eggs, beaten
- 1 teaspoon dry mustard
- 2 cups milk
- 1 pound bacon, fried and crumbled

Pout the melted butter in a 13 x 9-inch baking dish. Sprinkle the bread cubes evenly over the butter and sprinkle with 1 ½ cups of the cheese. In a medium bowl combine the eggs, mustard, and milk. Pour over the bread and cheese. Place the crumbled bacon on top of the egg mixture. Sprinkle with the remaining 1 cup cheese. Cover and place in the refrigerator overnight. The next morning preheat the oven to 325 degrees. Bake uncovered for 45 to 50 minutes.

Makes 8 to 10 servings.

Crescent Moon Cookies

I have been making these cookies for more than 50 years. When you find something good that people love, you will find yourself making the recipe again and again.

- ½ cup butter, softened
- 1 ¼ cups powdered sugar, divided
- 1 ½ cups all-purpose flour
- 1 teaspoon vanilla extract
- 1 cup finely chopped pecans

Preheat the oven to 325 degrees. Grease a cookie sheet and set aside. In a medium bowl add the butter and ¼ cup of the powdered sugar, stirring to mix well. Add the flour, vanilla, and pecans and mix well. The dough will be very stiff. Shape 1 tablespoon dough into a finger-size cookie and bend to give it a crescent shape. Place on the prepared cookie sheet. Bake for 12 to 15 minutes or until golden brown. Let cool and roll in remaining 1 cup powdered sugar.

Makes 2 dozen cookies.

Louise's Lemon Chooz

My sister Louise is one of the most generous and gracious ladies I have ever known. This recipe is just one of the many things I have her to thank for.

Lemon Chooz:
1 ½   cups all-purpose flour
½   cup butter, softened
½   cup firmly packed brown sugar
1   (14-ounce) can sweetened condensed milk
½   cup flaked coconut
½   cup chopped pecans

Lemon glaze:
1   cup powdered sugar
2   tablespoons lemon juice
1   tablespoon butter, melted

To make the Lemon Chooz: Preheat the oven to 350 degrees. Grease a 15 x 10 x 1-inch baking pan and set aside. In a small bowl place the flour, butter, and brown sugar. Using your fingers create a crumb consistency. Press into the prepared pan. Bake for 6 minutes and let cool for 15 minutes. Pour the condensed milk in a small bowl. Add the coconut and pecans and stir. Pour over the baked crust, spreading to the edges. Bake for 15 minutes. Cool for 15 minutes. **To make the lemon glaze**: In a small bowl combine the sugar, lemon juice, and butter. Drizzle over the cooled bars. Cut into squares.

Makes 34 squares.

Brown Sugar Apricot Casserole

This is an excellent side dish for pork.

5   (15-ounce) cans apricots, drained and divided
1   (12-ounce) box butter crackers, crushed and divided
1   pound light brown sugar, divided
¾   cup butter

Preheat the oven to 300 degrees. Butter a 13 x 9-inch baking dish. Layer ½ of the drained apricots in the baking dish. Cover with ½ of the cracker crumbs, ½ of the brown sugar, and ½ of the butter. Repeat the layers. Bake for 1 ½ hours.

Makes 12 servings.

Chocolate Mint Brownies

If there's anything better than curling up with a good book, it's curling up with a good book and this brownie.

Brownies:
- 2 (1-ounce) squares semisweet baking chocolate
- ½ cup butter
- 2 large eggs, well beaten
- 1 cup sugar
- ¼ teaspoon peppermint extract
- ½ cup all-purpose flour
- ⅛ teaspoon salt

Mint icing:
- 2 tablespoons butter, softened
- 1 cup powdered sugar
- 1 tablespoon heavy whipping cream
- ¼ teaspoon peppermint extract
- 3 drops green food coloring

Glaze:
- 1 (1-ounce) square semisweet baking chocolate
- 1 tablespoon butter

To make the brownies: Preheat the oven to 325 degrees. Grease a 9-inch-square baking dish. Bring the water in a double boiler to a boil and add the chocolate and butter to the bowl over the water. Stir over low heat until melted. Remove from the heat and let cool for 15 minutes. Add the eggs, sugar, peppermint extract, flour, and salt to the melted chocolate mixture. Mix well and pour into the prepared dish. Bake for 20 to 25 minutes or until firm. Let cool.

To make the mint icing: In a small bowl mix the butter, sugar, heavy cream, peppermint extract, and food coloring until creamy. Spread on top of the cooled brownies. Refrigerate the brownies while making the glaze.

To make the glaze: In a double boiler melt the chocolate and butter together over low heat. Stir to blend. Drizzle the glaze over the mint frosting. Refrigerate to set the chocolate.

Makes 2 dozen brownies.

Lemon Meringue Pie

You will notice that this recipe calls for fresh lemon juice. I know most cooks use bottled. Trust me and try this pie with fresh juice. I don't think you will ever go back to anything else.

Lemon pie:

1 ¼ cups sugar
½ cup cornstarch
¼ teaspoon salt
2 cups water
4 large eggs, separated
½ cup fresh lemon juice
¼ cup butter, softened
1 teaspoon lemon zest
1 (9-inch) baked piecrust

Meringue:

4 large egg whites
¼ teaspoon cream of tartar
½ cup sugar

To make the lemon pie: In a medium saucepan mix the sugar, cornstarch, and salt. Gradually add the water, stirring to mix well. Stir constantly over medium heat until the mixture has boiled for 1 minute. Remove from the heat. Place the egg yolks in a small bowl and beat until light. Stir ½ cup of the sugar mixture into the egg yolks, whisking until well blended. Add the lemon juice, butter, and lemon zest to the egg mixture and return to the saucepan. Over medium heat bring to a boil and boil for 1 minute, stirring constantly. Pour the mixture into the baked piecrust. Preheat the oven to 400 degrees.

To prepare the meringue: In a small bowl whip the egg whites and cream of tartar on high speed with an electric mixer until soft peaks form. Gradually add the sugar and continue beating until stiff peaks form. Spread the meringue over the pie filling, spreading to the edges to cover the hot filling. Bake for 8 to 10 minutes or until the meringue is lightly browned.

Makes 1 pie or 6 to 8 servings.

♥ CHAPTER 9 ♥

FESTIVALS

GOING TO TOWN

About the time the first leaf turned from green to gold in Fostertown, Retta started to worry. She was in charge of the Charity Cakewalk for the upcoming Fostertown Fall Festival, and she wanted everything to be just right. This year the proceeds were going to support the Fostertown Volunteer Firefighters, and Retta was determined to have the best desserts ever because her grandfather, God rest his soul, had been one of the first trained firemen in the county.

Now Mildred was calling to say she might not be able to come through after all. Her first grandchild was due to be born over in Richmond around the time of the Fostertown Fall Festival, and she was bound and determined to be there for the blessed event. She had thought that daughter of hers never would get married.

When Retta suggested that maybe Mildred could just make her famous coconut chiffon cake ahead of time and freeze it, Mildred sighed and hung up the phone. Retta could organize anything, that's why she was always head of the Charity Cakewalk Committee, but she couldn't find her way around a kitchen if you left her a trail of spatulas.

As for Mildred, you sure didn't want her volunteering for anything that required people skills. She could clear a room with that mouth of hers in less than ten seconds. But she could bake desserts that would break your heart they were so good. People always bought more Charity Cakewalk tickets if Mildred was donating one of her coconut chiffon cakes. More tickets meant more money for the firemen. (Please don't tell Retta you're concerned about the "gambling-like nature" of the cakewalk. She's been round and round about this with the pastors, and after careful discernment and lots of prayer, they all agree that because the money goes to a good cause, and the worst that can happen is someone gains a few pounds, it's not considered sinful. Not in the literal sense, anyway. If your conscience won't let you participate, fine. Just send Retta a check made out to Fostertown Volunteer Firefighters and she'll make sure you get a receipt for your taxes.)

♥

Across town, Micah Jones thought he might expire right there at the kitchen counter. This was his wife's first time to have an entry in the Charity Cakewalk, and for three weeks now she had been making desserts of all stripes and requiring him to sample her handiwork. So far he had consumed generous servings of such sugary concoctions as Strawberry Serenade, Raisin Rah-Rah, Luscious Low-Fat Lemon, and Fig Fiesta.

Now Micah loves his wife just as much as any other God-fearing, red-blooded American husband in Fostertown can be expected to. But he simply could not swallow one more bite. So he did something he hated to do, something he didn't even consider unless he was really tested. Micah Jones told a little white lie, yes he did.

"Mildred's coconut chiffon cake will be a mere memory once the fine people of Fostertown get a taste of your sweetness," said Micah. Now Micah knew this wasn't true, for his wife could not cook to save her life. Don't misunderstand Micah; his wife has many fine qualities. She can knit an afghan in the shape of your family crest in one weekend if you bring her the yarn before five on Friday afternoon. Every spring she volunteers to stay at the church all night for the Easter prayer vigil, when the deacon asks only that you sign up for a one-hour shift. Micah knows he's a lucky man. But if he had relied on his wife's cooking to keep him alive all these years, Micah would have long ago found himself six feet under with the rest of his people over on the hill at Faithful Pilgrim's Final Rest Cemetery.

Mrs. Jones notwithstanding—she was a wild card as far as Retta was concerned—Retta had to get busy calling the other Charity Cakewalk Committee members to take up the slack caused by Mildred's unfortunate scheduling snafu. She could probably count on her sister-in-law for another pecan pie, and quite possibly Eloise from the quilting group would bake an extra batch of her thumbprint cookies. Retta might have to promise Eloise she'd buy more Girl Scout cookies than usual from Eloise's granddaughter, but that was a small price to pay.

♥

As it is every fall, nothing brings Fostertown together like the festival. There are other events that get the residents excited, like the holiday musical at the middle school, and the library's semiannual book sale. But the fall festival is special. The annual gathering on the square is more than an opportunity to eat kettle corn and buy handmade brooms from the Lion's Club. It's a time for the citizens of Fostertown to share their little slice of heaven with folks from neighboring areas, and to honor a way of life that celebrates such fundamentals as family, tradition, and birdhouses made out of gourds. For some of us, there's no other way to live.

Two Bean Two Alarm Chili

There are hotter and spicier chili recipes out there. But this is by no means mild and has a little kick to it. I love the taste combination of the two beans.

1	pound ground beef
½	cup finely chopped onion
2	tablespoons chili powder
1	teaspoon cumin
1	teaspoon black pepper
1 ½	teaspoons salt
1	(4-ounce) can diced green chilies
1	(15-ounce) can tomato sauce
1	(15-ounce) can diced tomatoes
1	(15-ounce) can chili beans
1	(15-ounce) can pinto beans
1	cup water

Brown the ground beef in a large skillet over medium heat. Drain the fat. Add the onion and continue to cook for 3 minutes. Add the chili powder, cumin, black pepper, and salt. Continue to cook and stir for 3 more minutes. Transfer to a large Dutch oven. Add the green chilies, tomato sauce, diced tomatoes, chili beans, pinto beans, and water. Reduce the heat to low and simmer for 2 hours, stirring every 15 minutes, adding more water as necessary to reach the desired consistency.

Makes 6 to 8 servings.

Spicy Cheese Pita Crisps

This is a perfect accompaniment to soup. If you love spicy-hot, you might want to increase the amount of cayenne pepper.

4	cups shredded cheddar cheese
1 ½	cups butter, softened
⅔	cup grated Romano Cheese
½	teaspoon Worcestershire sauce
1	teaspoon minced garlic
1	teaspoon paprika
¼	teaspoon cayenne pepper
5	pita bread rounds

Preheat the oven to 350 degrees. In a large bowl combine the cheddar cheese, butter, Romano cheese, Worcestershire sauce, garlic, paprika, and cayenne pepper. Mix until creamy. Spread the cheese mixture on one side of each pita round and cut each into 4 wedges. Arrange the wedges on a baking sheet and bake for 10 to 12 minutes or until golden brown and crisp.

Makes 10 servings.

NOTE: If you have any leftover spread, save it to use on French bread.

Yes We Five Can Soup

A very hearty soup made especially for a cold, fall afternoon lunch.

1	pound ground beef
1	cup finely chopped onion
1	teaspoon salt
1	(15-ounce) can Veg-All
1	(14.5-ounce) can stewed tomatoes
1	(15-ounce) can Spanish rice
1	(10-ounce) can diced tomatoes with green chilies
1	(15-ounce) can creamed corn

Preheat a large saucepan over medium heat. When the pan is hot, add the ground beef, stirring until brown. Add the onion and salt and continue to cook for 3 minutes. Add the Veg-All, stewed tomatoes, rice, diced tomatoes with green chilies, and the creamed corn. Reduce the heat to low. Continue to simmer for 30 minutes, stirring occasionally.

Makes 6 servings.

Mrs. Eva's Strawberry Preserves

What makes this simple recipe special is the second step of pouring boiling water over the berries. It really helps preserve the color of the strawberries.

2 quarts firm ripe strawberries
6 cups sugar, divided

Wash and cap the strawberries and place in a large bowl. Pour enough boiling water over the strawberries to cover them by 1 inch. Let stand for 2 minutes. Drain strawberries and place in a large stockpot. Add 4 cups of the sugar and let come to a full boil over medium heat and cook for 2 minutes once the entire mixture is boiling. Add the remaining 2 cups sugar and continue to boil for 5 additional minutes, stirring occasionally. Pour into a shallow pan, making sure the mixture is not over 2 inches deep, and let stand overnight in a cool place.

Boil 4 pint jars and their lids. Pour the strawberry preserves into the hot jars, leaving ½-inch space at the top. Clean the rim of the jar and place the cap on the jar. Screw the lid band onto the jar. Allow the jars to cool for several hours.

Makes 4 pints.

NOTE: Great for gifts, but be sure to keep some for your family and guests.

Coconut Chiffon Cake

Yes, this cake is a lot of work. But trust me, it is worth it. I have tried a number of coconut cake recipes over the years, and this is the one I return to time and time again. I make at least a dozen of these every Christmas and this is the cake that people always ask me to make come charity auction time.

Cake:
- 2 large eggs, separated
- 1 ½ cups sugar, divided
- 2 ¼ cups all-purpose flour
- 3 teaspoons baking powder
- 1 teaspoon salt
- ⅓ cup vegetable oil
- 1 cup milk, divided
- 1 ½ teaspoons vanilla extract

Icing:
- 2 ¼ cups sugar
- ½ cup water
- 3 tablespoons light corn syrup
- 3 large egg whites
- 2 tablespoons powdered sugar
- 1 fresh coconut

To make the cake: Preheat the oven to 350 degrees. Grease and flour three 8-inch cake pans. Set aside. In a small bowl beat the egg whites with an electric mixer until soft peaks begin to form. Gradually add ½ cup of the sugar and continue to beat for 1 minute. In a medium bowl sift the remaining 1 cup sugar, flour, baking powder, and salt. Add the oil and ½ cup of the milk. Beat for 1 minute. Add the remaining ½ cup milk, egg yolks, and vanilla. Beat 1 more minute. Fold in the egg whites with a spatula.

Divide the batter among the 3 prepared cake pans. Bake for 20 minutes or until a toothpick inserted in the center of each cake comes out clean. Let the cakes cool in the pans for 10 minutes. Remove the cakes from the pans and place on waxed paper to continue to cool. Allow the cakes to cool completely before icing.

To make the icing: In a large saucepan mix the sugar, water, and light corn syrup together. Place over medium heat and cook until a soft ball forms, stirring occasionally until it reaches a temperature of 238 degrees. This should take 4 to 6 minutes.

While the sugar mixture cooks, add the egg whites to the bowl of a stand mixer and beat until soft peaks form. When the sugar mixture has reached the desired temperature, with the mixer running at medium speed, gradually add sugar mixture to the beaten egg whites. Continue to beat until all the syrup is incorporated into the egg whites. Continue to mix for 6 to 8 minutes until the icing is creamy and soft peaks form. Add the powdered sugar and mix for 1 additional minute.

Pierce the eye of the coconut with an ice pick and drain the coconut water into a small bowl. Crack the coconut shell, pry out the meat, and peel with a vegetable peeler. Grate the coconut meat with a fine grater.

To assemble the cake: Place one layer on the cake plate. Prick the layers with a fork and drizzle ⅓ of the coconut water over the layer. Place ⅓ of the icing on the first layer and frost the top and side. Sprinkle ⅓ of the grated coconut over the icing. Repeat the layers until finished. Cover and place in the refrigerator for at least 4 hours before serving.

Makes 1 cake or 12 to 14 servings.

NOTE: Keep refrigerated—if leftovers remain.

Sweet Peach Cake

This cake is wonderful for breakfast or brunch.

½	cup butter, softened
1 ½	cups firmly packed brown sugar
1	large egg
2	cups all-purpose flour
1	teaspoon baking soda
⅛	teaspoon salt
1	cup buttermilk
4	large ripe peaches, peeled and diced
¼	cup sugar
1	teaspoon cinnamon

Preheat the oven to 350 degrees. Grease a 13 x 9-inch baking dish and set aside. In a large bowl cream the butter and brown sugar until light and fluffy. Beat in the egg. In a small bowl sift the flour with the baking soda and salt. Alternately add the flour mixture and the buttermilk to the butter mixture, beating until smooth. Gently fold the peaches in. Pour into the prepared dish. Combine the sugar and cinnamon and sprinkle over the cake. Bake for 30 to 35 minutes.

Makes 16 servings.

Homemade Butter Pecan Ice Cream

I love homemade ice cream. One thing I am thankful to have lived to see is the invention of electric ice cream freezers. In the old days, you had to hand crank an ice cream freezer for at least thirty minutes. It was worth the hard work, but I am glad all I have to do now to enjoy this is to put the plug in the outlet.

1 ½	cups sugar
1 ½	cups egg substitute
1	(14-ounce) can sweetened condensed milk
1	quart light whipping cream
2	cups heavy whipping cream
⅛	teaspoon salt
½	teaspoon butter flavoring
2	cups chopped toasted pecans
1 to 2	quarts milk

Place the sugar and egg substitute in a medium bowl. Beat with an electric mixer on low speed for 3 minutes. Add the condensed milk and continue to beat. Add the light and heavy creams, salt, and butter flavoring. Continue to mix on low speed for 3 more minutes. Add the pecans and pour the mixture into an ice cream freezer's container. Add milk to the fill line. Freeze according to manufacturer's directions.

Makes 1 gallon.

School Days Chocolate Oatmeal Drop Cookies

I used to make these for my kids' lunches and they loved them.

- ½ cup butter
- ½ cup cocoa
- 2 cups sugar
- ½ cup milk
- 3 cups quick-cooking oatmeal
- ½ cup peanut butter
- 1 ½ teaspoons vanilla extract

In a large saucepan combine the butter, cocoa, sugar, and milk, stirring well. Let the mixture come to a full boil over medium heat and boil for 1 ½ minutes, stirring occasionally. Remove from the heat and add the oatmeal, peanut butter, and vanilla and stir until the peanut butter is incorporated. Drop by tablespoons onto a large sheet of waxed paper. Let cool and place in a covered container.

Makes 3 dozen cookies.

Homemade Vanilla Ice Cream

Everyone loves vanilla. But just in case you come across someone who doesn't, I've given you a few options that will help you make different flavors with ease.

    1 ½ cups egg substitute
    1   cup sugar
    1   (14-ounce) can sweetened condensed milk
    2   cups heavy whipping cream
    ⅛   teaspoon salt
    1   teaspoon vanilla extract
    ½   gallon milk

Place the egg substitute and sugar in the bowl of an electric mixer. Mix on high speed for 3 minutes. Add the condensed milk, whipping cream, salt, and vanilla. Continue to mix at medium speed for 3 minutes. Pour the mixture into your ice cream freezer's container and add the milk to the fill line. Freeze according to manufacturer's directions.

Makes 12 servings.

Variations: Stir the following ingredients into the vanilla ice cream before you place it in the ice cream freezer.

Peach or strawberry: add 1 quart of fruit sweetened with 1 cup of sugar.

Peppermint: Crush 8 ounces of peppermint candy. Add ½ teaspoon peppermint extract and 3 drops of red food coloring.

Easy Blackberry Cobbler

Serve this warm with vanilla ice cream on top.

5	cups fresh or frozen blackberries
1	cup water
1	cup all-purpose flour
1	cup sugar
1	teaspoon baking powder
½	teaspoon salt
¼	teaspoon cinnamon
1	large egg, slightly beaten
½	cup butter, melted

Preheat the oven to 350 degrees. Lightly spray an 11 x 9-inch baking dish with nonstick cooking spray. Spread the blackberries in the prepared baking dish. Add the water. In a small mixing bowl combine the flour, sugar, baking powder, salt, and cinnamon. Stir in the egg and mix until crumbly. Sprinkle over the berries. Drizzle the butter over the crumb mixture. Bake for 45 to 50 minutes or until golden brown.

Makes 6 to 8 servings.

Fresh Strawberry Pie

This is a simple Southern staple that every cook should know how to make.

3   tablespoons cornstarch
3   tablespoons strawberry gelatin
1   cup sugar
1   cup water
1   teaspoon red food coloring
1   quart strawberries
1   (9-inch) piecrust, baked and cooled
1   cup heavy whipping cream

In a small saucepan combine the cornstarch, gelatin, sugar, water, and food coloring. Bring to a boil over medium heat, stirring constantly, until the mixture is thick. Remove from the heat. Wash and cap the strawberries, draining well. Add the strawberries to the filling. Pour into the piecrust. Using a handheld electric mixer whip the heavy cream until soft peaks form. Top the strawberry pie with the whipped cream.

Makes 1 pie or 6 to 8 servings.

Seven-Layer Bars

This is an easy recipe to use to teach your children and grandchildren how to make delicious desserts.

½   cup butter, melted
1 ¼   cups graham cracker crumbs
1 ¼   cups sweetened coconut flakes
1   cup semisweet chocolate chips
1   cup butterscotch chips
1   cup chopped walnuts
1   (14-ounce) can sweetened condensed milk

Preheat the oven to 350 degrees. Place the melted butter in a 13 x 9-inch baking dish. Sprinkle the graham cracker crumbs evenly over the butter. Sprinkle with the coconut. Add a layer of chocolate chips, butterscotch chips, and walnuts. Pour the condensed milk evenly over the mixture. Bake for 30 minutes. Let cool and cut into 24 squares.

Makes 24 servings.

Coconut Glazed Pound Cake

I like to make this cake to have on hand when unexpected company stops by for coffee.

Cake:
- 2 cups cake flour
- ½ teaspoon salt
- 1 ½ teaspoons baking powder
- 1 cup vegetable oil
- 2 cups sugar
- 5 large eggs
- ¼ cup milk
- 1 teaspoon vanilla extract
- 1 teaspoon coconut flavoring
- 1 cup shredded coconut

Glaze:
- 1 cup sugar
- ½ cup milk
- ¼ cup butter
- 1 teaspoon coconut flavoring

To make the cake: Preheat the oven to 325 degrees. Grease and flour one 10-inch tube cake pan. Set aside. In a medium bowl sift together the flour, salt, and baking powder. In a medium bowl cream the oil and sugar for 1 minute with an electric mixer. Add the eggs one at a time, beating well after each addition. Add the flour mixture a small amount at a time. Add the milk, vanilla, coconut flavoring, and shredded coconut, mixing well. Pour into the prepared tube pan and bake for 1 hour or until a toothpick inserted in the center comes out clean. Let the cake sit in the pan for 10 minutes before transferring to a serving plate.

To prepare the glaze: In a small saucepan combine the sugar, milk, butter, and flavoring. Place over medium heat and boil for 3 minutes, stirring constantly. Pour directly on the cake and let drizzle over the sides.

Makes 16 servings.

BeBe's Pear Bread

This sweet bread is perfect to wrap up and take to a bake sale.

3	cups all-purpose flour
2	cups sugar
1	cup chopped pecans
¼	teaspoon baking powder
½	teaspoon cinnamon
¼	teaspoon ground cloves
¼	teaspoon nutmeg
1	teaspoon baking soda
½	teaspoon salt
¾	cup canola oil
2	cups grated pears (2 large pears)
3	large eggs, slightly beaten
2	teaspoons vanilla extract

Preheat the oven to 350 degrees. Grease and flour two 9 x 5 x 3-inch loaf pans. Set aside. In a large bowl add the flour, sugar, pecans, baking powder, cinnamon, cloves, nutmeg, baking soda, and salt. Stir to combine. Make a well in the center of the dry ingredients. Add the oil, pears, eggs, and vanilla. Stir until just moistened. Pour into the prepared loaf pans. Bake for 50 to 55 minutes, or until a toothpick inserted in the center comes out clean.

Makes 2 loaves or 24 servings.

NOTE: If you are making this recipe for yourself, it is wonderful served with cream cheese.

Pecan Pie

Every Southern cook has to know how to make a pecan pie. Period. This is one of the best I have ever eaten.

3	large eggs
⅔	cup sugar
1	cup light corn syrup
2	teaspoons all-purpose flour
¼	cup butter, melted
1	teaspoon vanilla extract
1 ¼	cups pecan halves
1	(9-inch) unbaked piecrust

Preheat the oven to 350 degrees. In a medium bowl add the eggs and sugar. Blend well using a whisk. Stir in the corn syrup, flour, butter, vanilla, and pecans. Pour into the piecrust and bake for 50 minutes.

Makes 1 pie or 6 to 8 servings.

Fresh Florida Orange Pie

My brother-in-law enjoyed this pie at someone's home in Florida in the 1960s. He loved it so much he brought the recipe back to me. For almost 50 years, this has been one of my signature dishes.

Crust:

- 4 large eggs, separated (whites used for crust)
- ¼ teaspoon cream of tartar
- 1 cup sugar
- ¼ cup chopped pecans or walnuts

Filling:

- 4 egg yolks from eggs separated for crust
- ½ cup sugar
- ⅛ teaspoon salt
- 2 tablespoons lemon juice
- 1 teaspoon grated orange rind
- 6 large navel oranges, peeled and sectioned, divided
- 2 cups heavy whipping cream

To make the crust: Preheat the oven to 275 degrees. Butter a 9-inch deep-dish pie pan. In a large bowl beat the egg whites with the cream of tartar until soft peaks form. Gradually add the sugar. Continue beating until the sugar is completely dissolved, about 5 minutes. Spread the egg whites in the prepared pie pan, making a nest. Sprinkle with the nuts. Bake for 1 ½ hours or until the crust feels dry to the touch.

To make the filling: In the top of a double boiler mix the egg yolks, sugar, salt, lemon juice, and orange rind. Cook over medium heat, stirring constantly for about 8 minutes. Remove from the heat and carefully add ¾ of the orange sections. In a medium bowl add the heavy cream and beat with a handheld electric mixer until soft peaks form. Fold ½ of the whipped cream into the filling. Add to the baked pie shell. Top the pie with the remaining whipped cream. Garnish with the remaining orange sections. Refrigerate for 4 hours.

Makes 1 pie or 8 servings.

Yellow Cake with Caramel Icing

Unfortunately, making a yellow cake from scratch is becoming a lost art. This traditional Southern cake is one I hope everyone tries. It really is delicious.

Cake:
- 3 cups all-purpose flour
- 2 cups sugar
- 1 tablespoon baking powder
- ½ teaspoon salt
- 1 ½ cups milk
- ½ cup butter, softened
- 2 large eggs
- 1 ½ teaspoons vanilla extract

Caramel icing:
- 1 pound firmly packed light brown sugar
- 3 tablespoons all-purpose flour
- ¾ cup cold water
- ½ cup butter
- 1 pound powdered sugar
- 1 teaspoon vanilla extract

To make the cake: Preheat the oven to 350 degrees. Grease and flour two 9 x 1 ½-inch round cake pans and set aside. In a large bowl add the flour, sugar, baking powder, and salt, stirring to combine. Add the milk and butter and beat with an electric mixer on low speed for 2 minutes. Add the eggs and vanilla and beat on high speed for 2 more minutes. Pour into the prepared pans. Bake for 25 to 30 minutes or until a toothpick inserted near the center comes out clean. Remove from the oven and cool 10 minutes. Remove from the pans and allow to cool completely before icing.

To prepare the icing: In a large saucepan mix the brown sugar, flour, water, and butter. Place over medium heat and bring to a boil to dissolve the brown sugar. Reduce the heat to low and cook until the temperature registers 234 degrees on a candy thermometer, stirring occasionally until a soft ball forms. Remove from the heat and let stand 10 minutes without stirring. Add the powdered sugar and vanilla, beating until the mixture reaches a spreading consistency. One tablespoon of hot water may be added if the icing becomes too stiff. Frost the top and sides of each cake layer.

Makes 1 cake or 16 servings.

Peanut Butter Cookies

These cookies not only taste wonderful, but the aroma from your oven fills the house with homemade goodness.

½   cup butter, softened
½   cup sugar
½   cup firmly packed brown sugar
½   cup peanut butter
1   large egg
1 ½   cups all-purpose flour
1   teaspoon baking soda
⅛   teaspoon salt
1   teaspoon vanilla extract

Preheat the oven to 350 degrees. Grease a large cookie sheet and set aside. In a large bowl cream the butter, sugar, brown sugar, and peanut butter until smooth. Add the egg and mix well. In a small bowl combine the flour, baking soda, and salt together and add to the creamed mixture. Add the vanilla and mix well.

Scoop the cookie dough 1 tablespoon at a time and roll into a ball. Place each cookie on the prepared cookie sheet 2 inches apart. Flatten with a fork or the bottom of a glass. Bake 8 to 10 minutes. Transfer to a cooling rack to cool.

Makes 2 dozen cookies.

♥ CHAPTER 10 ♥

LENDING A HAND

BECAUSE IT'S JUST WHAT WE DO

Avery Proctor did not like feeling helpless. Ever since her teen years, when her daddy left her momma and she had to step in to take care of her baby sisters, Avery had promised herself she would grow up strong so she wouldn't have to rely on strangers for help. For the most part, that's the way things worked out. She put her two children through college, buried a husband too young, and sent more than one suitor packing because no one measured up to her beloved Harry.

A few times along the way, Avery had to ask for assistance. But not often, and not without repaying what she borrowed, with interest—and a handwritten thank-you note. So she knew about giving and receiving, about how sometimes it takes just a little bit extra to get somebody through a rough spell.

Avery was extra sensitive to people in need, and it just about broke her heart when she saw sad stories on the evening news. She wanted to save each and every person in distress. Most times, of course, she couldn't do anything more than weep, and pray, and send a check to the American Red Cross, like with 9/11 and Katrina. Those two tragedies liked to do her in. So when the waters rose in Tennessee in 2010 in what that cute young weatherman called a "five-thousand-year flood," Avery was ready.

Well, she was sort of ready. Her basement got four feet of water in it, so she lost her daughters' old prom dresses and some grapevine wreaths she was planning to decorate for the holiday craft fair at the church, but she was lucky and she knew it. Avery felt bad that she couldn't save the people who drowned or rebuild the homes of those who lost everything. Goodness knows she would have been willing to wield a hammer if her doctor hadn't told her to let up on the manual labor after that time she got tangled in the barbed wire trying to mend a section of fencing by herself. But Avery could do one thing to help: she could cook.

As soon as the grocery store reopened after the worst of the rains had passed, Avery loaded up her cart with all the ingredients she needed for her specialties: bacon cornbread and cold spaghetti salad. She was halfway to the checkout line when she decided she'd make some grape tea, too, and maybe a few chocolate fried pies.

Avery had been famous for her bacon cornbread ever since she first took a batch to the annual cemetery working more than twenty years ago. Now she would cook all day and all night, as long as it took, to serve the people of her community who had been there for her when she needed them after Harry died. For starters, she would drive her station wagon across town and leave baskets of food for the Marshall brothers, who had lost everything, and the Newtons, whose son had moved them into a hotel until their house could be repaired. She would pour iced tea into Mason jars until every thirsty neighbor had a drink.

It wouldn't even matter to Avery if she got her dishes back; not this time, even though she's a stickler for proper etiquette, just like her Aunt Gracie. She wouldn't complain if she didn't receive thank-you notes or if no one called to sing her praises. Instead, Avery would be grateful that this time, when tragedy came calling, she was able to answer with her hands and her heart.

Breakfast Hot Chocolate

You can enjoy this all day long.

- ½ cup sugar
- ⅓ cup unsweetened cocoa powder
- ⅛ teaspoon salt
- ½ cup water
- 3 ½ cups milk
- ¼ teaspoon vanilla extract
  Marshmallows (optional)
  Whipped cream (optional)

In a medium saucepan stir together the sugar, cocoa powder, and salt. Stir in the water. Bring to a boil over medium heat, stirring constantly. Add the milk and vanilla. Heat to the boiling point, but do not boil.

To serve: Pour into serving cups and add marshmallows or top with whipped cream if desired.

Makes 4 servings.

Percolator Gold Punch

Tastes as good as it smells. This is a great early morning alternative to coffee on a cool fall day.

- 4 cups pineapple juice
- 1 (12-ounce) can apricot nectar
- 4 cups apple cider or apple juice
- 1 cup orange juice
- 1 cinnamon stick
- 1 teaspoon whole cloves

In a 20-cup percolator combine the pineapple juice, apricot nectar, apple cider, and orange juice. Place the cinnamon stick and cloves in the basket. Perk through a regular coffee cycle. Place in an insulated bottle to keep hot.

Makes 12 to 14 servings.

Brown Sugar Brownies

One of my favorite places on earth—the Greenbrier in West Virginia—serves a version of this brownie at tea every afternoon. Your volunteers will thank you if you make this for an afternoon snack.

- 1 ½   cups butter
- 1 ½   pounds dark brown sugar
-   5   large eggs
-   4   cups all-purpose flour
- 3 ½   teaspoons baking powder
-   ¾   teaspoon salt
-   1   (10-ounce) package butterscotch chips
- 1 ½   cups chopped pecans

Preheat the oven to 350 degrees. Grease and flour a 15 x 10 x 2-inch baking pan and set aside. In a 2-quart saucepan melt the butter and brown sugar over low heat. Remove from the heat and add eggs one at a time, beating until well incorporated. In a large bowl sift together the flour, baking powder, and salt. Add to the egg mixture. Add the butterscotch chips and pecans and pour the mixture into the prepared baking pan. Bake for 25 to 30 minutes or until golden brown and firm to the touch.

Makes 2 dozen brownies.

Jalapeño Bacon Corn Bread

I could make a meal out of just this corn bread. It's that good.

        3   cups self-rising cornmeal
    2 ½   cups milk
        3   eggs, beaten
        1   cup finely chopped onion
    1 ½   cups grated cheddar cheese
        ¼   pound bacon, fried and crumbled
        ¼   cup diced pimientos
        2   tablespoons sugar
        1   cup creamed corn
        ½   cup vegetable oil
        2   jalapeño peppers, finely chopped

Preheat the oven to 400 degrees. Grease a 13 x 9-inch pan and set aside. In a large bowl mix together the cornmeal, milk, eggs, onion, cheese, bacon, pimientos, sugar, corn, vegetable oil, and peppers. Pour the batter into the prepared pan and bake for 30 to 40 minutes or until golden brown.

Makes 16 servings.

Sauerkraut Relish

The fact that this recipe has sugar in it and is served cold makes it unlike any sauerkraut you have ever tried. It tastes great on a hot dog.

        1   (15-ounce) can chopped sauerkraut, undrained
        ½   cup finely chopped onion
        ½   cup finely chopped celery
        ½   cup finely chopped red bell pepper
        ⅔   cup sugar
        ⅔   cup apple cider vinegar

In a large bowl combine the sauerkraut, onion, celery, and pepper and mix well. In a small saucepan place the sugar and vinegar. Bring to a boil over medium heat, stirring occasionally. Pour the hot mixture over the sauerkraut mixture. Cover and chill in the refrigerator for 4 hours before serving.

Makes 6 to 8 servings.

Watermelon Salsa

This is a great side dish served alongside barbecue and corn bread.

- 8 cups diced watermelon
- 2 cups diced cantaloupe
- 2 cups diced honeydew
- 1 medium cucumber, peeled, seeded, and diced
- ⅓ cup finely chopped red onion
- 4 jalapeños, seeded and finely chopped
- ⅓ cup fresh lime juice
- ⅓ cup firmly packed brown sugar

In a large bowl mix together the watermelon, cantaloupe, honeydew, cucumber, onion, and jalapeños. In a small bowl combine the lime juice and brown sugar, stirring to dissolve the brown sugar. Pour over the melon mixture and lightly stir.

Makes 12 servings.

NOTE: This salsa is also delicious with chips, as any good salsa should be.

Red Potato Salad

Leave your potato peeler in the drawer for this one.

- 3 pounds red potatoes, washed but unpeeled
- 4 large eggs, boiled and chopped
- ¼ cup chopped red onion
- 1 cup chopped dill pickles
- 1 cup mayonnaise
- 1 tablespoon mustard
- 1 teaspoon apple cider vinegar
- 1 teaspoon salt

In a large saucepan place the potatoes, cover with water by 1 inch, and bring to a boil over medium heat. Cook for 30 minutes or until tender. Drain the water. Let the potatoes cool slightly. Dice the potatoes. In a large bowl add the diced potatoes, eggs, onion, pickles, mayonnaise, mustard, vinegar, and salt. Mix to coat the potatoes. Place in a serving bowl. Cover and refrigerate until time to serve.

Makes 8 to 10 servings.

Baked Fruit with Coconut Topping

This is a tasty and beautiful side dish. It's a wonderful addition to pork or chicken.

1 (15-ounce) can peach halves, drained
1 (15-ounce) can pear halves, drained
1 (15-ounce) can apricot halves, drained
1 (20-ounce) can sliced pineapple, drained (reserve ½ cup juice)
½ cup butter
2 tablespoons all-purpose flour
1 cup firmly packed brown sugar, divided
½ cup chopped pecans
½ cup flaked coconut

Preheat the oven to 350 degrees. Grease a 13 x 9-inch casserole dish. Layer the peaches, pears, apricots, and pineapple in the casserole dish and set aside. In a small saucepan melt the butter over medium heat. Add the flour to the melted butter, stirring constantly for 2 minutes. Add the reserved pineapple juice and ½ cup of the brown sugar. Bring to a boil, stirring constantly. Pour the mixture over the fruit. Sprinkle with the remaining ½ cup of the brown sugar and the pecans. Top with the coconut. Bake for 30 minutes.

Makes 10 to 12 servings.

Black-eyed Peas with Tomatoes

This is a new twist on one of the most Southern of all vegetables.

- 3 slices bacon, diced
- 1 cup finely chopped onion
- ½ cup finely chopped green bell pepper
- ½ cup finely chopped celery
- 1 (15-ounce) can stewed tomatoes, chopped
- ½ teaspoon dried basil
- 2 teaspoons sugar
- ½ teaspoon salt
- ½ teaspoon black pepper
- 1 (16-ounce) bag frozen black-eyed peas

In a large skillet fry the bacon until crisp. Set the bacon aside to drain. Reserve the drippings. In a medium saucepan place the reserved bacon drippings and over medium heat add the onion, bell pepper, and celery, stirring for 3 minutes. Add the tomatoes, basil, sugar, salt, black pepper, and black-eyed peas. Simmer over low heat for 1 ½ hours. Add water as necessary. Top with the cooked bacon.

Makes 8 servings.

White Beans with Bacon and Tomato Sauce

White beans have always been a Southern delicacy. I took this to a family reunion last year and had five people ask for the recipe and one cousin ask to take the leftovers home.

Beans:
- 1 cup dried white beans
- 6 cups water plus water to cover beans while soaking
- 1 medium carrot, cut into 1-inch pieces
- 1 medium onion, coarsely chopped
- 2 teaspoons coarse salt

Bacon and tomato sauce:
- 4 slices bacon, diced
- ¼ cup olive oil
- 1 cup finely chopped onion
- 2 tablespoons minced garlic
- 1 teaspoon coarse salt
- 2 (15-ounce) cans petite chopped tomatoes
- 2 teaspoons fresh chopped thyme (1 teaspoon dried)

To prepare the beans: In a large saucepan place the beans, cover with 2 inches of water, and soak overnight. Drain. Add the beans back to the pan and add the 6 cups of water. Bring the beans to a boil. Add the carrot and onion. Simmer over low heat partially covered for 45 minutes, until the beans are almost done. Add the salt, continuing to cook for about 45 minutes, until the beans are tender. Discard the carrot. Drain the beans in a colander, reserving 1 ½ cups of the bean liquid for the bacon and tomato sauce.

To make the bacon and tomato sauce: Cook the bacon in a heavy skillet over medium heat, stirring until crisp. Add the olive oil and onion, stirring for 10 minutes. Add the garlic and salt and continue to cook for 2 minutes. Add the tomatoes and chopped thyme. Reduce the heat to low and simmer for 45 minutes or until the sauce is thickened, stirring occasionally.

Return the beans to the large saucepan. Add the tomato sauce and the 1 ½ cups of reserved bean juice. Simmer uncovered for 45 minutes.

Makes 10 servings.

NOTE: This can be made a day ahead and placed in the refrigerator. To reheat, place over low heat for 30 minutes. Thin with water while reheating, if necessary.

Cold Spaghetti Salad

Great served alongside a sandwich.

    4   quarts water
    1   tablespoon salt
    1   pound spaghetti, broken into 2-inch pieces
   12   slices bacon, diced and cooked until crisp
    ½   cup finely chopped celery
    1   cup finely chopped onion
    1   cup finely chopped green bell pepper
    ½   cup sliced green olives
    2   large tomatoes, chopped
    ⅓   cup salad seasoning mix
    1   (16-ounce) bottle Italian salad dressing
    ½   cup grated Parmesan cheese

In a large stockpot bring 4 quarts of water to a boil. Add the salt and spaghetti and cook for 8 to 10 minutes or until al dente. Drain. In a large bowl, combine the spaghetti, bacon, celery, onion, bell pepper, olives, tomatoes, salad seasoning, Italian dressing, and Parmesan cheese. Toss to coat. Chill 2 hours before serving.

Makes 8 to 10 servings.

Grilled Baby Back Ribs

A lot of people are intimidated by cooking ribs. It does take a little work to master, but boy is it worth it when you do.

¼ cup paprika
2 teaspoons onion powder
2 teaspoons garlic powder
1 tablespoon salt
1 teaspoon red cayenne pepper
2 teaspoons black pepper
4 to 6 pounds baby back ribs
  Barbecue sauce

In a small bowl mix the paprika, onion powder, garlic powder, salt, cayenne pepper, and black pepper. Rub the mixture over the ribs, coating evenly. Grill over indirect heat for 5 to 6 hours, turning every 30 minutes. Be sure to keep the lid on the grill. If you are using charcoal you will need to add more charcoal during the cooking process. Baste with your favorite barbecue sauce during the last 15 minutes of cooking.

Makes 6 to 8 servings.

NOTE: A good hostess knows to take along some wet naps too, especially when you are eating these ribs outdoors.

Fried Barbecue Chicken

If there's anything more Southern than fried chicken, it's got to be this fried barbecue chicken.

- 1 (3- to 4-pound) chicken, cut into serving pieces
- 2 teaspoons salt, divided
- ½ teaspoon black pepper
- 1 cup all-purpose flour
  Oil for browning the chicken
- ½ cup finely chopped onion
- 2 tablespoons Worcestershire sauce
- ¼ teaspoon cayenne pepper
- ¼ teaspoon chili powder
- 1 teaspoon dry mustard
- 1 cup tomato juice
- ½ cup water
- 2 tablespoons firmly packed brown sugar
- 2 teaspoons paprika
- ¼ cup ketchup
- ¼ cup apple cider vinegar

Preheat the oven to 350 degrees. Grease a 13 x 9-inch baking dish and set aside. Season the chicken with 1 teaspoon of the salt and the ½ teaspoon pepper. Place the flour in a shallow dish and dredge the chicken in the flour to coat. In a 10-inch skillet heat the oil until a pinch of flour sizzles when dropped in the skillet. Brown the chicken in batches. Transfer fried chicken to the prepared baking dish.

In a medium saucepan add the onion, Worcestershire sauce, cayenne pepper, chili powder, mustard, tomato juice, water, brown sugar, paprika, the remaining 1 teaspoon salt, ketchup, and vinegar. Simmer over medium heat for 10 minutes. Pour over the chicken, cover, and bake for 1 hour. Remove the cover and continue to bake for 30 more minutes.

Makes 6 to 8 servings.

Tennessee Goo Goo Pie

Like the commercial says, "It's good."

- ½ cup butter
- 2 ounces semisweet chocolate
- 1 cup sugar
- ½ cup all-purpose flour
- 2 large eggs, slightly beaten
- 1 teaspoon vanilla extract
- ¼ teaspoon salt
- 2 Goo Goo candy bars, chopped

Preheat the oven to 325 degrees. Grease a 9-inch pie pan and set aside. In a small saucepan melt the butter and chocolate over low heat. Add the sugar and flour and mix well. Remove from the heat and add the eggs, vanilla, and salt. Pour into the prepared pie pan and bake for 15 to 20 minutes. Sprinkle with the chopped Goo Goo bar and return to the oven. Bake for 10 minutes.

Makes 1 pie or 6 to 8 servings.

Breakfast Cups

So easy to make and take.

- 1 (16-ounce) can flaky biscuits
- 1 (8-ounce) package cream cheese, softened
- 3 large eggs
- ½ pound sausage, browned, crumbled, and drained
- 2 cups shredded cheddar or Swiss cheese

Preheat the oven to 375 degrees. Grease two 12-cup muffin tins. Separate each biscuit into 3 pieces. Press each piece into a muffin cup. In a large bowl beat the cream cheese and eggs together until smooth. Stir in the sausage and cheese. Divide mixture equally among the muffin cups. Bake for 10 to 15 minutes, until firm to the touch and golden brown.

Makes 18 servings.

VARIATION: Substitute ½ pound bacon, fried and crumbled, for the sausage.

Jerome Bars with Butter Cream Frosting

This will appeal to both adults and kids.

Jerome bars:

20	whole (2 ½ x 5-inch) graham crackers, divided
¾	cup melted butter
1	cup sugar
1	large egg
½	cup evaporated milk
1	cup graham cracker crumbs
1	cup flaked coconut
1	cup chopped pecans

Butter cream icing:

6	tablespoons butter, softened
3	cups powdered sugar
1	teaspoon vanilla extract
3	tablespoons milk or light whipping cream

To make the Jerome bars: Break each graham cracker in half and place in the bottom of a 13 x 9-inch pan, breaking crackers when necessary to form 1 layer in the pan. In a medium saucepan add the butter, sugar, egg, and evaporated milk, mixing well. Bring to a boil over medium heat. Add the graham cracker crumbs, coconut, and pecans and continue to cook for about 3 minutes or until slightly thickened. Remove from the heat and spread over the crackers. Place the remaining graham crackers over the filling.

To make the butter cream icing: In a small bowl cream the butter and sugar until smooth. Add the vanilla and milk and continue stirring until the mixture becomes a spreading consistency. Spread over the Jerome bars.

Makes 24 servings.

NOTE: Keep refrigerated.

Butter Pecan Cupcakes

I love taking cupcakes to outdoor events. No knives, plates, or forks are needed.

Cupcakes:
- 1 cup chopped pecans
- ½ cup plus 3 tablespoons butter, divided
- 1 ¼ cups sugar
- 2 teaspoons vanilla extract
- 2 large eggs
- 2 cups all-purpose flour
- 1 ½ teaspoons baking powder
- ¼ teaspoon salt
- ⅓ cup milk

Pecan icing:
- 3 cups powdered sugar
- ¼ cup milk
- 4 tablespoons butter, softened
- ½ teaspoon vanilla extract
- ⅓ cup toasted pecans, saved from the cupcake recipe

To make the cupcakes: Preheat the oven to 350 degrees. Place the pecans in a baking dish and dot with 3 tablespoons of the butter. Toast for 8 to 10 minutes, stirring often. Remove from the oven to cool. Preheat the oven to 375 degrees. Prepare two 12-cup muffin tins with paper liners and set aside.

In a medium bowl combine the sugar, the remaining ½ cup butter, and vanilla and mix until light and creamy. Add the eggs one at a time, beating well after each addition. In a small bowl stir together the flour, baking powder, and salt. Alternately add the flour mixture and milk to the butter mixture. Fold in the toasted pecans, reserving ⅓ cup of the pecans for the frosting. Fill the muffin cups ½ full. Bake for 20 minutes or until a toothpick inserted in the center comes out clean. Allow to cool completely before icing.

To make the pecan icing: In a large bowl combine the powdered sugar, milk, butter, and vanilla. Beat with an electric mixer until smooth. Fold in the pecans.

Makes 24 cupcakes.

Chocolate Fried Pies

So Southern. So good. And you can use this pastry for your fruit-filled fried pies as well.

Pastry:
5	cups all-purpose flour
1	tablespoon salt
1	tablespoon sugar
1	cup vegetable shortening
1	large egg, slightly beaten
1	(13-ounce) can evaporated milk
	Vegetable oil for frying

Chocolate filling:
1 ½	cups sugar
3	tablespoons cocoa
¾	cup all-purpose flour
1 ½	cups milk
6	tablespoons butter
2	teaspoons vanilla extract

To create the pastry: In a large bowl combine the flour, salt, sugar, and shortening. Use a pastry blender to mix the dry ingredients and the shortening together. Add the egg and evaporated milk and mix to form the dough. Place the dough in the refrigerator for 30 minutes.

To make the chocolate filling: In a medium saucepan combine the sugar, cocoa, and flour. Add the milk and place over medium heat to cook. Let the mixture come to a boil, continue to stir and cook for 2 minutes until it thickens. Add the butter and vanilla. Place a piece of plastic wrap the size of the pan over the mixture. Let cool completely before making the pies.

To assemble the pies: Roll the pastry out on a lightly floured board to a ¼-inch thickness. Cut into 6-inch circles. Place 1 tablespoon of the chocolate filling in the center of each circle. Brush the top half of the circle with a few drops of water, fold the pastry in half, and press the edges together with a fork. Prick the top with a fork before frying.

Preheat a medium skillet with ½-inch of oil over medium heat. Test the oil by dropping a piece of dough into the oil. If the dough starts dancing you're ready to fry. Fry each pie 3 minutes, or until browned. Turn over and fry 3 minutes on the other side. Remove to paper towels to drain.

Makes 2 dozen fried pies.

♥ CHAPTER 11 ♥

COMFORT FOOD

ALL HAIL
THE COVERED DISH

Most times, the best thing you can do for someone who is grieving is offer to listen. Lending an ear does more than you might imagine. Quite often, though, the next best thing you can do for someone who is grieving is to offer to bring food.

Growing up in Mississippi, I was introduced at a young age to the idea that food serves as a tangible expression of sympathy. When news of death came to my family's home—be it a neighbor, church member, friend, or business associate of my father's—Mother's response was, "What can I bring?"

So I learned early on about the assignment of duties, the scheduling of deliveries, and which foods freeze best for reheating later. Polling friends and neighbors to find out who had time to bake a casserole and who had eggs on hand to whip up a pound cake. Who could take something over to the family right away, and which person could drop off a full meal later in the day, closer to suppertime. How to affix a piece of masking tape with my name on it to the bottom of a glass dish, so the recipient would know who should get the thank-you note and where the 13 x 9-inch pan needed to be returned in a timely manner.

I sensed, seemingly without being taught, the comfort that a covered dish could provide for someone who had little interest in eating. But the heart and soul of such culinary kindness was made real for me when my own father died some ten years ago.

As Mother and I returned home from the hospital on that awful Monday afternoon in September we noticed something hanging from the knob of the back door. Inside that plastic bag were a spiral ham, a loaf of sourdough bread, and a jar of honey mustard. The sight of that dangling pork caused me to burst into tears. Now I knew my father was really dead, because friends had already started bringing food.

The sandwiches Mother and I ate that night kept us going until morning, when we went to meet my sisters at Wright and Ferguson Funeral Home to make my father's final arrangements. It sounds like a simple thing, and it was: meat and bread. But it was also concern and sympathy and love. And for two sad women—on that particular night, in that particular kitchen—it might as well have been manna from heaven.

♥

After my father's burial, family and friends gathered at a cousin's house not far from St. Peter's Cemetery in Oxford. There was pink cake and fried chicken, biscuits and smoked meats, congealed salad with mayonnaise on top. Stuffed eggs with and without paprika. Sweet tea served in etched glasses that had touched generations of my family's lips.

I circled the dining room table like a woman who had been starved for days. As I put yet another forkful of food into my mouth, I began to feel guilty about my gluttony. How could I eat so much when my precious father was dead? But the food served a twofold purpose. It nourished my physical body, which had been drained by the unexpected death and drawn-out days of funeralizing. And sharing the food with my kinfolk, who had lovingly prepared the smorgasbord, replenished my spirits as well.

In the trying months after my father's death, there were days, of course, when Mother and I could not eat a bite because we were too busy crying and remembering. But on those occasions when we were hungry, craving food but also connection, we had only to open the door to the extra freezer in the laundry room. Nestled on the frost-covered wire shelves, in all their aluminum-foiled glory, were sausage and wild rice, pork loin, and gumbo. Yeast rolls and cheese bread and cakes. The knowledge that someone had cared enough to prepare food for us warmed our hearts as we heated the dishes according to the directions on the index cards taped to the containers. These gifts—which is what we considered them to be—strengthened Mother and me when we thought we might not survive our loss. Lonely nights were made more tolerable through such tangible offerings of comfort, because at least we did not have to worry about feeding ourselves. We had enough to contend with as we tried to imagine our lives without the man who had been the center of our family's universe.

It's now been a decade since I lost my father, the first love of my life, and I can still remember, in a few instances at least, who brought which food to our home. In some ways, those Pyrex dishes and cookie sheets continue to sustain me today. Because long after the food has been consumed, the memories remain.

"Putting on the Ritz" Corn Casserole

If you look up "Southern church lady casseroles" in the dictionary, this is the recipe you will find. It's been around for years, and for good reason. People love it.

2   (14-ounce) cans whole kernel corn, drained
1   (14-ounce) can French-style green beans, drained
1   (10.75-ounce) can cream of mushroom soup
1   cup sour cream
¼   cup chopped onion
¼   cup chopped celery
1   sleeve (36 crackers) Ritz crackers, crushed
½   cup melted butter

Preheat the oven to 350 degrees. Grease a 13 x 9-inch baking dish and set aside. In a large bowl combine the corn, green beans, soup, sour cream, onion, and celery. Mix well. Pour the vegetable mixture into the prepared baking dish. In a medium bowl mix the crushed crackers and melted butter. Sprinkle over the top of the casserole and bake for 30 minutes.

Makes 10 servings.

Ms. King's Chess Pie

I have tried many different chess pie recipes. When I discovered this one more than thirty years ago, my search for the perfect chess pie was over.

1   stick margarine or butter
1 ½   cups sugar
1   tablespoon apple cider vinegar
3   large eggs
1   teaspoon vanilla extract
1   9-inch piecrust, unbaked

Preheat the oven to 400 degrees. In the top of a double boiler place the margarine or butter and melt. Add the sugar and vinegar. In a small bowl beat the eggs and then strain into the butter and sugar mixture, stirring well. Add the vanilla. Remove from the heat and pour into the piecrust. Bake for 10 minutes. Reduce the heat to 350 degrees and continue baking for approximately 45 minutes or until firm to the touch.

Makes 1 pie or 6 to 8 servings.

Harmony Hominy Casserole

Truth be told, yellow and white hominy don't taste all that different. But using both colors adds visually to this traditional Southern casserole.

1 tablespoon vegetable oil

1 cup finely chopped onion

1 teaspoon minced garlic

1 (15-ounce) can white hominy, drained

1 (15-ounce) can yellow hominy, drained

1 cup shredded cheddar cheese

1 (4-ounce) can chopped green chilies

¾ cup sour cream

½ teaspoon cumin

½ teaspoon salt

Preheat the oven to 350 degrees. Grease or spray a 2-quart baking dish and set aside. In a large skillet heat the oil over medium heat. Sauté the onion and garlic until translucent. Add both cans of hominy, the cheddar cheese, green chilies, sour cream, cumin, and salt. Mix well and pour into the prepared baking dish. Bake for 20 minutes or until bubbly.

Makes 8 servings.

Mrs. Bryant's Dinner Rolls

Mrs. Bryant was my high school English teacher. Not only was she a gracious and kind woman, but she was also a great cook. This recipe is quite old, yet it produces what I think are the best Southern dinner rolls you can find.

½   cup sugar
1   teaspoon salt
½   cup vegetable shortening
1   cup boiling water, divided
1   package active dry yeast
3   cups all-purpose flour, divided
1   large egg, slightly beaten

In the bowl of your stand mixer place the sugar, salt, and shortening. Add ¾ cup of the boiling water so the shortening begins to soften. Allow the remaining ¼ cup of the water to reach lukewarm temperature. Add the yeast to the lukewarm water and stir to dissolve. Let rest for 3 minutes.

Add 1 cup of the flour to the sugar mixture. Use the mixer to combine well. Add the yeast mixture and the second cup of flour and mix well. Add the remaining cup of flour and mix well. Add the egg and continue to beat with the mixer for about 15 minutes or until the dough leaves the side of the bowl. Cover and let rise until dough doubles in bulk. Punch down and place in lightly greased bowl, turning to grease the top also. Cover and refrigerate overnight.

When ready to roll out, place the dough on a floured board and knead lightly. Roll out to ½-inch thick. Form into desired shapes or cut with a 2-inch biscuit cutter. Grease muffin tins or a cookie sheet and place dough ¼ inch apart. Butter the tops. Leave in a warm place to rise for approximately 3 hours. Preheat the oven to 400 degrees and bake for 20 minutes.

Makes 3 dozen rolls.

Swiss Potato Bake

There are a number of different potato dishes in this book, but at the end of the day I have to admit this one is my favorite.

1 ½   teaspoons salt
1   teaspoon garlic powder
1   teaspoon lemon pepper seasoning
¼   teaspoon cayenne pepper
3   pounds red potatoes, peeled and thinly sliced, divided
2   cups shredded Swiss cheese, divided
4   tablespoons butter, divided
2   cups canned chicken broth

Preheat the oven to 450 degrees. Butter a 13 x 9-inch baking dish and set aside. In a small bowl mix the salt, garlic powder, lemon pepper seasoning, and cayenne pepper. Place ½ of the potato slices in the prepared baking dish and sprinkle with ½ of the mixed dry seasoning. Place 1 cup of the Swiss cheese on top and dot with 2 tablespoons of the butter. Repeat with the remaining potato slices and the rest of the dry seasoning. Top with the remaining 1 cup Swiss cheese. Pour the chicken broth over the top and dot with the remaining 2 tablespoons butter. Bake for approximately 1 hour or until golden brown.

Makes 6 to 8 servings.

Broccoli Salad with Sunflower Seeds

This salad is great year round, but with fresh broccoli available during the winter months when some other vegetables aren't, I tend to make it more when it's cold outside.

Dressing:

- 1 cup mayonnaise
- ½ cup sugar
- 2 tablespoons apple cider vinegar

Broccoli salad:

- 6 cups broccoli florets, washed and trimmed
- 1 cup golden raisins
- ¼ cup finely chopped red onion
- 1 cup shredded cheddar cheese
- 6 slices crisp-fried bacon, crumbled
- ½ cup sunflower seeds

To prepare the dressing: In a small bowl combine the mayonnaise, sugar, and vinegar. Mix well. Set aside while you prepare the salad.

To prepare the salad: Cut the broccoli into bite-size pieces and place in a large bowl. Add the raisins, onion, and cheese to the broccoli. Pour the dressing over the mixture. Toss gently to mix. Cover and chill until ready to serve.

To serve: Sprinkle the broccoli salad with the crumbled bacon and sunflower seeds.

Makes 10 servings.

Farmhand Beans

When I was growing up my mother would say that someone with a hearty appetite ate like a farmhand—meaning they had worked up an appetite by doing hard work. That name is appropriate for this dish, because it will satisfy the hungriest people you know.

   4   slices bacon, diced
   ½   pound ground beef
   ¼   cup chopped onion
   ½   pound Polish sausage, cut into ¼-inch-thick slices
   1   (15-ounce) can pork and beans
   1   (15-ounce) can black beans, drained
   ½   cup ketchup
   ¼   cup firmly packed brown sugar
   2   tablespoons molasses
   1   teaspoon Worcestershire sauce
   2   teaspoons prepared mustard
   ½   teaspoon salt
   ½   teaspoon black pepper
   ¼   teaspoon ground cumin

In a large skillet fry the bacon until brown and crisp. Drain and set aside. Discard the bacon drippings. Using the same skillet, brown the ground beef and onion. Add the Polish sausage and brown lightly. In a large saucepan, combine the pork and beans, black beans, ketchup, brown sugar, and molasses and mix well. Stir in the Worcestershire sauce, mustard, salt, pepper, and cumin. Add the beef mixture and bacon to the bean mixture. Simmer for 30 minutes on medium heat, stirring occasionally.

Makes 10 servings.

Country Fried Chicken

There is no mood that can't be lifted by a good piece of fried chicken.

- 1 (3- to 4-pound) chicken, cut into serving pieces
- 2 cups buttermilk
- 2 teaspoons salt
- 1 teaspoon black pepper
- 1 teaspoon paprika
- 1 ½ cups self-rising flour
  Vegetable shortening for frying

Place the chicken pieces in a large nonreactive bowl, cover with the buttermilk, and place in the refrigerator for at least 6 hours. Drain the chicken and season with the salt, pepper, and paprika. Add the flour to a large plastic or paper bag. Add the chicken and shake until the pieces are thoroughly coated.

Preheat a deep fryer to 325 degrees and fry the chicken pieces for 15 minutes. Or place 1 ½ inches of oil in a large cast-iron skillet and over medium heat fry the chicken pieces for 15 minutes, until golden brown, turning once. The chicken is done when the juices run clear.

Makes 4 to 6 servings.

Bank Tea

This tea has been served in the executive dining rooms of the South's best banks for decades. I say if it's good enough for their million-dollar customers, it's good enough for my friends and loved ones.

- 6 single-size tea bags
- 2 ¼ cups sugar
- 4 cups boiling water
- 6 ounces frozen orange juice concentrate
- 6 ounces frozen lemonade concentrate
- 1 liter ginger ale
- 4 cups water

Place the tea bags and sugar in a gallon container. Add the boiling water and let steep for 20 minutes. Remove the tea bags. Add the orange juice and lemonade concentrates. Add the ginger ale and 4 cups of water. Keep refrigerated.

Makes 8 servings.

NOTE: If you do not want to add ginger ale to this tea, add an additional 4 cups of water.

Meatloaf with Tomato Gravy

You can also bake this in a tube or Bundt pan and serve with mashed potatoes in the center for a festive look.

Meatloaf:
- 2 pounds ground beef
- 2 large eggs, slightly beaten
- 1 cup milk
- 3 tablespoons ketchup
- 2 tablespoons minced onion
- 1 tablespoon salt
- ½ teaspoon black pepper
- 1 cup soft bread crumbs
- ½ cup grated cheddar cheese
- 2 strips bacon

Tomato gravy:
- 2 tablespoons vegetable shortening
- 2 tablespoons all-purpose flour
- 1 ½ cups tomato juice
- ¼ teaspoon salt
- ¼ teaspoon black pepper

To make the meatloaf: Preheat the oven to 350 degrees. Grease a 9 x 5 x 3-inch loaf pan and set aside. In a large bowl add the ground beef, eggs, milk, ketchup, onion, salt, and pepper. Mix well. Fold in the bread crumbs and the cheese. Place in the prepared pan, cover with the strips of bacon, and bake for 1 hour.

To make the tomato gravy: In a small saucepan over medium heat place the shortening. Add the flour and stir for 2 minutes. Add the tomato juice, salt, and pepper, stirring constantly for about 5 minutes or until thickened. Serve on top of the meatloaf or alongside it.

Makes 8 servings.

Roast Pork Loin with Fresh Mushroom Sauce

This dish is simple to make and so delicious.

Roast pork:
- 1 (3-pound) boneless pork loin, trimmed
- 1 teaspoon dried thyme
- 2 teaspoons salt
- 1 teaspoon black pepper

Fresh mushroom sauce:
- ⅓ cup apple juice
- 1 cup chicken broth
- 1 cup heavy cream
- 2 tablespoons butter
- 8 ounces fresh mushrooms, sliced

To make the roast: Preheat the oven to 450 degrees. Grease a 13 x 9-inch baking dish. Sprinkle the roast with thyme, salt, and pepper. Place in the prepared baking dish and roast for 20 minutes. Reduce the oven temperature to 325 degrees. Continue roasting for an additional 1 ½ hours. Transfer the pork to a serving platter. Reserve the pan drippings. Tent the meat with aluminum foil while you make the sauce.

To prepare the sauce: In a medium saucepan combine the reserved pan drippings, apple juice, chicken broth, and heavy cream. Bring to a boil over medium heat. Cook for 20 minutes or until the mixture thickens, stirring frequently. In a small skillet melt the butter and sauté the mushrooms until tender. Add to the sauce.

Makes 8 servings.

NOTE: Serve the sauce in your grandmother's gravy boat.

Slow-cooked Oven Barbecued Brisket

As good as this is right out of the oven, it is just as good two or three days later. This is a perfect Bless Your Heart dish.

¼ cup Worcestershire sauce
1 ½ cups ketchup
½ teaspoon Tabasco sauce
½ cup sugar
1 teaspoon celery salt
1 (4-pound) beef brisket, trimmed
1 tablespoon salt
2 teaspoons black pepper
12 buns

Preheat the oven to 275 degrees. Grease a 13 x 9-inch baking dish and set aside. In a small saucepan combine the Worcestershire sauce, ketchup, Tabasco sauce, sugar, and celery salt. Place over low heat, stirring constantly until the sugar dissolves. Pour ½ of the sauce into the prepared baking dish. Sprinkle the beef with the salt and pepper and place on top of the sauce in the baking dish. Top the beef with the remaining sauce. Cover and roast for 5 hours, or until very tender. When ready to serve, cut diagonally across the grain into thin slices.

To Serve: Serve on buns with sauce from the pan.

Makes 12 servings.

Pink Cake

Pretty to look at and pretty delicious too!

Cake:
- 1 cup vegetable shortening
- 2 cups sugar
- 6 large eggs
- 1 (3-ounce) package strawberry gelatin
- 1 teaspoon vanilla extract
- 1 teaspoon salt
- 1 teaspoon butter flavoring
- 1 teaspoon baking powder
- 3 cups all-purpose flour
- 1 cup light whipping cream

Glaze:
- ½ cup frozen strawberries, thawed and drained
- ¼ cup butter, softened
- ½ teaspoon vanilla extract
- 1 ½ cups powdered sugar

To make the cake: Preheat the oven to 300 degrees. Grease and flour a 10-inch Bundt cake pan and set aside. In a medium bowl cream the shortening and sugar with an electric mixer. Add the eggs one at a time, beating well after each addition. Add the gelatin, vanilla, salt, butter flavoring, and baking powder. Alternately add the flour and cream, beginning and ending with the flour. Pour the batter into the prepared Bundt pan. Bake for 1 hour or until cake tester comes out clean. Let cool for 10 minutes. Transfer to a cake plate.

To make the glaze: In a medium bowl combine the strawberries, butter, vanilla, and powdered sugar. Drizzle over the cooled cake.

Makes 16 servings.

German Chocolate Pie

Don't make this pie unless you want it to become something you make regularly. Once people have tried this, they will ask you to make it again and again.

Filling:
- ⅓ cup sugar
- 3 tablespoons cornstarch
- 1 ½ cups milk
- 1 (4-ounce) German chocolate bar
- 2 large eggs, slightly beaten
- 1 tablespoon butter
- 1 teaspoon vanilla extract
- 1 (9-inch) piecrust, baked

Topping:
- ½ cup sugar
- 1 egg, beaten
- ⅔ cup evaporated milk
- ¼ cup butter
- 1 ⅓ cups sweetened canned coconut
- ½ cup chopped pecans

To make the filling: In a medium saucepan combine the sugar, cornstarch, and milk. Add the chocolate bar. Cook over medium heat, stirring until the chocolate bar melts and bubbles form around the edge of the pan. Remove from the heat. In a small bowl beat the eggs. Add 1 cup of the chocolate mixture to the eggs to temper, and then add back to the chocolate mixture in the saucepan. Continue to cook until the mixture thickens, stirring constantly. Remove from the heat and add the butter and vanilla. Pour into the baked piecrust.

To make the topping: In a medium saucepan combine the sugar, egg, evaporated milk, and butter. Cook over medium heat, stirring constantly until thick. This should take about 6 minutes. Remove from the heat and add the coconut and pecans. Spread over the chocolate pie.

Makes 1 pie or 6 to 8 servings.

NOTE: This pie can be eaten warm or covered and placed in the refrigerator and served chilled.

Mary Beth's Strawberry Cheesecake Trifle

This cake is good anytime of the year, but it's the perfect Southern summertime dessert.

- 1 quart fresh strawberries
- 1 cup sugar, divided
- 1 pound cream cheese, softened
- 1 (12-ounce) carton frozen whipped topping, thawed
- 1 (10-ounce) pound cake loaf, cut into 1-inch cubes
- 1 (4.25-ounce) Hershey's bar, grated

Wash the strawberries, remove the caps, and slice. In a large bowl add the strawberries and ½ cup of the sugar, stir well, and set aside. In a large bowl beat the cream cheese and the remaining ½ cup sugar until blended. Fold in the whipped topping. Place ½ of the pound cake in a trifle or serving bowl. Top with ½ of the strawberries, ⅓ of the cream cheese mixture, and ⅓ of the grated chocolate. Repeat the layers. Top with the remaining cream cheese and garnish with the remaining grated chocolate. Cover and refrigerate for 4 hours.

Makes 16 servings.

Red and Green Grape Salad

Southerners care about appearances. Trust me, this salad tastes as good as it looks.

- 2 pounds seedless green grapes
- 2 pounds seedless red grapes
- 1 (8-ounce) package cream cheese
- 1 cup sour cream
- 1 (8-ounce) package marbled cheddar cheese, grated
- ½ cup sugar
- ½ cup firmly packed brown sugar
- 1 cup chopped pecans

Wash the grapes and remove the stems. Let dry on a dish towel while preparing the cheese mixture. In a large bowl combine the cream cheese, sour cream, cheddar cheese, and sugar. Add the grapes, stirring to coat them. Place in a 13 x 9-inch glass serving dish. In a small bowl mix the brown sugar and pecans. Sprinkle over the top of the grape salad. Cover with plastic wrap and place in the refrigerator overnight.

Makes 16 servings.

Extra Credit Chocolate-Caramel-Layer Squares

My son had a teacher in high school who would give him extra credit when he brought these delicious brownies to share with the class. They are that good.

1   (14-ounce) bag caramels
⅔   cup evaporated milk, divided
1   (18-ounce) package German chocolate cake mix
¾   cup butter, softened
1   cup pecans, chopped
1   cup semisweet chocolate chips

Preheat the oven to 350 degrees. Grease a 13 x 9-inch baking dish and set aside. In the top of a double boiler combine the caramels and ⅓ cup of the evaporated milk. Cook over medium heat until the caramels are completely melted. Remove from the heat. In a large bowl combine the cake mix, the remaining ⅓ cup evaporated milk, butter, and pecans, mixing until everything is incorporated. The dough will be stiff. Divide the dough in half and press half in the prepared baking dish. Bake for 6 minutes.

Remove from the oven and sprinkle with the chocolate chips. Pour the caramel mixture over the chocolate chips. Press the remaining cake dough on a piece of waxed paper the size of the baking dish. Place on top with dough side down and peel the paper away. Cook for 16 minutes. Cool for 30 minutes. Allow the caramel layer to harden in the refrigerator for 1 hour before cutting into 24 slices.

Makes 2 dozen brownies.

Quick Cola Cake

This is a much quicker and easier version of the traditional Cocola Cake.

Cake:

- 1 (18-ounce) package butter fudge cake mix
- 1 (3-ounce) package instant vanilla pudding mix
- 3 large eggs, slightly beaten
- 1 cup vegetable oil
- 1 teaspoon vanilla extract
- 1 cup cola
- 1 ½ cups miniature marshmallows

Icing:

- ½ cup butter
- 1 pound powdered sugar
- 3 tablespoons cocoa
- ⅓ cup cola
- 1 cup chopped pecans

To make the cake: Preheat the oven to 350 degrees. Grease a 13 x 9-inch baking dish. In a large bowl combine the cake and pudding mixes, eggs, oil, and vanilla. Blend with a hand mixer until just moistened. Add the cola gradually, beating at medium speed for 4 minutes. Fold in the marshmallows. Pour into the prepared baking dish. Bake for 25 minutes.

To make the icing: In a small saucepan melt the butter over low heat. Add the sugar, cocoa, and cola. Mix well. Add the pecans and spread the icing over the warm cake.

Makes 16 servings.

ACKNOWLEDGMENTS

My heartfelt appreciation to the family and friends who served as fodder for the essays in this book, whether they know it or not. To Bryan Curtis, my gratitude for hanging on to my phone number all those years; and to Patsy Caldwell, my admiration for reminding me what it means to be Southern.

Amy Lyles Wilson

I have always considered it a blessing to be able to not only cook for the nourishment of my family and friends, but also that I was able to do so professionally for more than forty years.

As the youngest of nine children, I am thankful to my brothers and sisters, their spouses and children. I come from a family of wonderful cooks, and some of the best recipes in this book come from my family. Three of my nieces, Roberta Tidwell, Jan Metcalf, and Donna Allen have been especially inspiring to me and have contributed to my love of cooking. My cousin Tom Allen has always believed in me and always pays an unbelievable price for my coconut cakes at various fund-raisers.

In my professional life I was blessed to have been able to cook for tens of thousands of appreciative people. To the fine people at the Dickson County Board of Education and Ingram Industries, I offer my sincere thanks for your kind words and encouragement. A special thanks goes to Christine Steele, Noah Daniel, Rhonda Cook, Joann Holder, Robert Hardin, and the entire Ingram family, especially Martha Ingram and the late E. Bronson Ingram. From the beginning, my biggest supporter has probably been Betty Lou Wolcott. She was the first person to ever hire me to cater a party and remains one of the classiest Southern women I have had the good fortune to know.

A final word of thanks to some very special friends. John Egerton, for inspiring me with his writing about Southern food. Jean Smith, the best neighbor and taster anyone could hope for. Mike, Jamie, and Claire Monroe Sims, for allowing me to be such a part of their lives. Luanne and Ronny Greer for offering support in every way you can possibly imagine it. And to my new friend Amy Lyles Wilson, I have so loved working with you on this project. To all the good people of Charlotte, Tennessee, I thank you for your love and support. And finally to the women of the Water Tower Cooking Class: Donna Brown, Sue Drinnen, Betsy Duke, Cynthia Marvin, Judy Nicks, Judy Redden, Betty Nicks Smith, Sue Smith, Gay Taylor, and especially Sara Caudill. Thank you for your friendship and allowing me to share my love of cooking with you.

Bless your hearts,
Patsy Caldwell

ABOUT THE AUTHORS

Writer AMY LYLES WILSON was born and raised in Jackson, Mississippi. Now based in Nashville, Tennessee, Wilson wrote the text for the *New York Times* bestselling cookbook *Cooking with Friends*, and her essay "The Guts to Keep Going," about helping her mother adjust to widowhood, was featured on National Public Radio's "This I Believe" and appears in *This I Believe II: More Personal Philosophies from Remarkable Men and Women* (Henry Holt, 2008). Wilson holds academic degrees from Millsaps College, the University of Mississippi, and Vanderbilt University Divinity School. An affiliate of Amherst Writers and Artists, she leads writing workshops on such topics as creativity, spirituality, and grief. You can find her at www.amylyleswilson.com.

PATSY CALDWELL is the owner of Watertower Food Concepts, a cooking school in Charlotte, TN. She has been a culinary professional for more than forty years.

INDEX